COOKING FOR YOUR FREEZER

COOKING FOR YOUR FREEZER

Mary Shepherd

CONTENTS

Published exclusively for
Marks and Spencer p.l.c. in 1983
by Octopus Books Limited
59 Grosvenor Street
London W1

© 1983 Hennerwood Publications Limited

ISBN 0 86273 064 3

Printed in Hong Kong

INTRODUCTION

Many freezer books give detailed guidance on choosing and maintaining a freezer, and full instructions for preparing individual foods. This book concentrates on the recipes suitable for freezing and en route gives reminders of the important rules. There are 5 chapters which will provide you with ideas for all occasions. The cooking time in the recipes refers to the time required to prepare each dish for the freezer and not for serving. This will be noted in the serving instructions.

Soups are best stored in their concentrated state, they take less space, and adding the milk or cream when reheating improves the finished taste and texture.

The freezer can hold a stock of light meals and snacks which can be quickly reheated.

Dishes for entertaining can be prepared when you have time to enjoy making them and be confident of the end result.

Use the freezer for good standby family meals, made with economy cuts or special bargain offers of meat and poultry. Fish, too, when seasonal can be prepared and frozen away for a variety of dishes.

The freezer makes a perfect storehouse for gluts of seasonal fruits that can be combined with pastry or puréed. Experiment with exotic flavours of icecreams. A small batch of choux pastry yields many buns which will provide several puddings.

Freezing Prepared Food
Freezing is the best and most natural way of preserving food. *But* it is essential to use good ingredients, prepare them correctly, and package and store them carefully. Here are a few reminders of the basic rules.

Recipes prepared for freezing should be cooled as quickly as possible after cooking. Do not put hot food into the freezer as it will cause excess ice crystals and raise the temperature of other foods around it.

Seasoning
Always keep salt and pepper to a minimum during the preparation of dishes for the freezer as flavours develop during storage and seasoning tends to become concentrated on reheating. Taste and adjust the seasoning just before serving. Highly seasoned or spiced foods are therefore better after a short storage time, about 1 month, particularly those flavoured with garlic and curry.

Storage
As a rule, prepared dishes in the freezer should be used within 3 months, during which there will be no significant change in flavours. However, there are some foods which are better stored for only 1 month, oily fish, for example, and dishes containing cured meats. Freezing tends to affect the flavour of the fat in these dishes so that they develop rancid off-flavours.

Packaging
Rigid polythene containers with close-fitting lids are suitable for most foods. Square shapes take less space than round ones. Emptied and cleaned ice cream or catering size margarine containers are ideal. Make use of large yogurt pots and margarine tubs provided they have tight-fitting lids.

Aluminium foil containers with fitting lids can be used safely with many foods. However, recipes containing garlic and pieces of onion, i.e. most pâtés, or dried fruit, can cause the foil to dissolve and discolour the food. To prevent this happening use a protective wrapping of cling film or greaseproof paper.

Polythene freezer bags are useful for overwrapping or for foods that have been 'open frozen'. Use the thicker gauge freezer bags not those you get free from supermarkets that have holes in them. Always seal bags securely with a tie. Cling film, freezer film and foil are all good wrapping materials. Use cling film as protective wrapping as mentioned above or for any foods sprinkled with salt or lemon juice. Freezer film is thicker, has a greater strength and gives more protection. It can be used on its own. Foil is malleable and easily formed around awkwardly shaped food. It makes a good barrier for strong flavours, but does tear readily. Use a layer of cling or freezer film inside the foil or put the foil parcel into a freezer bag. Do not rely on foil alone for anything with sharp bones, pad them first with freezer film or greaseproof paper.

Do not freeze and store food in glass dishes, unless they are made of 'freezer-to-oven' material. This will be stated on the labelling of the dish. There are a variety of polythene containers which are suitable for freezing and pretty enough to be used as serving dishes.

Freezer-to-oven casseroles, earthenware or cast iron dishes are all suitable for preparing main meals for freezing. In most cases thawing is recommended before reheating, to allow the dish and the food to be brought nearer to room temperature before it is put into a hot oven. If you are short of dishes turn the food out after freezing (loosen it with a palette knife or quickly dip the dish into hot water), and wrap the food separately. Alternatively you can line the dish with foil before you cook the dish, freeze and then release the container from the foil. If you have a microwave oven, remember that you cannot use metal or foil containers for reheating.

Labelling and Storing

This is very important as once frozen, many foods lose much of their identity. Use stick-on freezer labels for packages, cartons or pots. Write on the freezer bags or containers with a chinagraph pencil. Secure bags with a tie and label. Write the labels with coloured pens or use coloured labels for different food groups. If other members of the family will be taking food out of the freezer and finishing the cooking, mark the label, for example, 'add 150 ml (¼ pint) milk'; or 'sprinkle with grated cheese' and place under a medium hot grill until golden brown.

Organizing the Freezer

Keeping the freezer well organized is essential, so that you have a record of the contents, you are aware of what needs replenishing and you use food in the correct rotation.

For the chest freezer, use large coloured polythene bags, one for each food group, or fill the freezer with cardboard boxes that fit snugly together. Put coloured sticky tape round the top of the boxes for the food groups. Use baskets for small items for immediate use. Baskets can be made-to-measure for your freezer. There are several manufacturers who do this and who advertise in the freezer magazines. Because the baskets fit the freezer dimensions exactly, they prevent ice crystals forming on the inside walls of the case, and make the freezer work more economically.

If you have an upright freezer there is no room for baskets or cardboard boxes. Allocate each shelf a particular food group and label the food carefully. Keep a record of the items on each shelf and remember to keep the book near the freezer for easy reference.

Thawing

For most recipes, thawing is recommended before final cooking or reheating, either in the refrigerator or at room temperature. If you have a microwave oven use the 'defrost' setting. However, pastry is best frozen raw and cooked just before serving, usually from frozen. Brush with beaten egg just before cooking, rather than before freezing.

If you prefer to make and serve the recipes without freezing, the following instructions may help: To serve cold, chill in the refrigerator until required. To serve hot, complete the cooking as given in the serving instructions for each recipe. In recipes where the food is cooked after freezing, follow the serving instructions, using the same oven temperature and reduce the cooking time by about one third. This applies mainly to pastry dishes. If necessary cover the pastry with foil to prevent it becoming too brown while the filling cooks through.

Garnishes and Decoration

Garnishes and decorations are best added just before serving, to avoid being crushed by wrapping or during storage.

SOUPS AND STARTERS

CHICKEN MINESTRONE

900 ml (1½ pints) chicken stock
1 ham knuckle bone, stripped of most meat
1 medium onion, peeled and chopped
2 carrots, scraped and sliced
2 sticks celery, thinly sliced
100 g (4 oz) cooked chicken meat, chopped
100 g (4 oz) short macaroni
100 g (4 oz) frozen peas
½ teaspoon dried oregano or marjoram (optional)
salt
freshly ground black pepper
grated Parmesan cheese, to serve

Preparation time: 10 minutes
Cooking time: 20 minutes

1. Put the stock into a large saucepan with the ham bone, onion, carrots and celery. Bring to the boil, then simmer for 20 minutes.
2. Remove the ham bone; cut off and chop any meat. Return to the soup with the chicken meat. Cool.
To Freeze: Put the soup into a rigid freezer container, cover and freeze.
To Serve: Place in a large saucepan and bring slowly to the boil, stirring occasionally. Add the macaroni, peas and herb (if using) and simmer for 10 minutes or until the macaroni is tender. Add salt and pepper. Serve with grated Parmesan cheese.

MELON AND GRAPE COCKTAIL

750 g (1½ lb) melon
100 g (4 oz) black grapes, halved and seeded
4 tablespoons red grape juice
8 tablespoons tonic water

Preparation time: 10 minutes

1. Remove the seeds and skin from the melon and cut the flesh into dice.
2. Mix with the grapes and pour over the grape juice.
To Freeze: Put into a rigid freezer container, cover and freeze.
To Serve: Allow to thaw in the refrigerator for 6-8 hours. Spoon into glass dishes and pour the tonic water over the fruit just before serving.

BROWN BEEF STOCK

Makes about 1.75 litres (3 pints)
1 kg (2 lb) beef bones
50 g (2 oz) beef dripping
1 onion, peeled and chopped
1 stick celery, chopped
1 carrot, scraped and chopped
2 bouquets garni
salt
freshly ground black pepper

Preparation time: 10 minutes
Cooking time: 2¾ hours
Oven: 220°C, 425°F, Gas Mark 7

For ease of use, pack the stock in 600 ml (1 pint) quantities for freezing. Alternatively, freeze as ice cubes, then pack in a freezer bag.

1. Wash the bones and put into a large saucepan. Cover with water, bring to the boil and simmer for 5 minutes. Drain.
2. Put the bones into a roasting tin with the dripping and place in a preheated oven. Cook for 40 minutes, turning the bones over once.
3. Return the drained bones to the large saucepan and add the vegetables, bouquets garni, salt and pepper. Cover with water. Bring to the boil, cover and simmer for 2 hours.
4. Strain the stock into a large bowl and leave until cold. Skim the fat from the surface and use as dripping.
To Freeze: Put the stock into rigid freezer containers or ice cube trays, cover and freeze.
To Serve: Use for soups, stews and casseroles, or for making gravy.
Cubes may be added, still frozen, to hot soups, and then brought back to the boil.

Variation:
White Chicken Stock: Use the carcass from a roasted chicken. Proceed from Step 3.

ABOVE: Chicken minestrone; BELOW: Melon and grape cocktail

RED PEPPER AND TOMATO SOUP

40 g (1½ oz) butter, melted
1 tablespoon oil
1 medium onion, peeled and chopped
350 g (12 oz) tomatoes, chopped
225 g (8 oz) red peppers, cored, deseeded and chopped
1 tablespoon plain flour
¼ teaspoon dried basil
salt
freshly ground black pepper
450 ml (¾ pint) water
150 ml (¼ pint) half-cream or milk
chopped parsley, to garnish

Preparation time: 10 minutes
Cooking time: 45 minutes

CREAMY CABBAGE SOUP

50 g (2 oz) butter
350 g (12 oz) hard white cabbage, cored and shredded
150 ml (¼ pint) chicken stock
300 ml (½ pint) milk
salt
white pepper
chopped chives or spring onion tops, to garnish

Preparation time: 10 minutes
Cooking time: 40 minutes

This basic soup is delicious as it is, but it also lends itself to many cooked vegetable additions, such as sliced button mushrooms, chopped asparagus tips, peas and carrots, and sweetcorn, or chopped cooked ham. It is worth making double or treble quantity to put away in the freezer.

1. Melt the butter in a saucepan, add the cabbage and mix together. Cover with a well-fitting lid and cook very gently, stirring occasionally, for about 30 minutes or until the cabbage is very soft.
2. Add the stock. Process in an electric blender until smooth and creamy.
To Freeze: Put into a rigid freezer container, cover and freeze.
To Serve: Place in a saucepan and slowly bring to the boil, stirring occasionally. Add the milk, and salt and pepper to taste. Serve garnished with chopped chives or spring onion tops.

It is necessary to sieve the soup even after processing in an electric blender to remove the skins of the peppers and tomatoes.

1. Melt the butter with the oil in a saucepan. Add the onion and fry gently until soft but not coloured. Stir in the tomatoes and red peppers and cook for a further 5 minutes.
2. Add the flour, basil, salt, pepper and water. Bring to the boil, stirring. Cover and simmer for 30 minutes.
3. Process the soup in an electric blender, then rub through a sieve. Allow to cool.
To Freeze: Put in a rigid freezer container, cover and freeze.
To Serve: Place in a saucepan and slowly bring to the boil, stirring occasionally. Just before serving, add the cream or milk and reheat but do not boil. Taste and adjust the seasoning. Serve garnished with chopped parsley.

FROM THE LEFT: Creamy cabbage soup;
Red pepper and tomato soup; Soda bread

SODA BREAD

Makes 1 loaf

225 g (8 oz) wholemeal flour
1 teaspoon salt
1 teaspoon bicarbonate of soda
1 teaspoon sugar
25 g (1 oz) butter
250 ml (8 fl oz) milk
1 tablespoon white vinegar

Preparation time: 10 minutes
Cooking time: 45 minutes
Oven: 190°C, 375°F, Gas Mark 5

If you can obtain it, use 200 ml (⅓ pint) buttermilk instead of the milk and vinegar. Do not be surprised that the mixture is stickier than the usual texture of a bread dough.

1. Sift together the flour, salt and bicarbonate of soda. Add the sugar and rub in the butter.
2. Stir together the milk and vinegar and add. Mix to a soft, slightly sticky dough.
3. Put into a lightly greased 18 cm (7 inch) diameter cake or sandwich tin. Smooth the surface and cut a cross in the top of the dough.
4. Place in a preheated oven and bake for about 45 minutes or until risen and browned and sounds hollow when tapped on the bottom. Turn out of the tin and cool on a wire tray.
To Freeze: Wrap in foil and freeze.
To Serve: Allow to thaw at room temperature for about 2 hours. Serve cold or warmed, with butter.

LITTLE POTS OF PÂTÉ

100 g (4 oz) streaky bacon, rind removed and chopped
225 g (8 oz) turkey or chicken livers, chopped
1 hard-boiled egg
1 clove garlic, peeled and crushed
2 tablespoons brandy
1 tablespoon double cream
pinch of dried thyme
pinch of ground mace
salt
freshly ground black pepper
To garnish:
2 hard-boiled eggs, separated
sprigs of parsley

Preparation time: 10 minutes
Cooking time: 15 minutes

Chicken and turkey livers are very cheap and readily available from supermarkets. They are perfect for making this simple and delicious pâté.

1. Fry the bacon lightly in a frying pan until the fat runs. Add the livers and cook for 10 minutes, stirring occasionally.
2. Put into an electric blender, add the rest of the ingredients with salt and pepper to taste, and process to a smooth purée.
To Freeze: Put into freezerproof ramekin dishes, cover and freeze.
To Serve: Allow to thaw in the refrigerator for 6-8 hours. Chop the egg white finely and sieve the egg yolk. Arrange in rings on top of the pâté with a parsley sprig in the centre. Serve with hot toast.

BLUE CHEESE SOUFFLÉS

Serves 6
50 g (2 oz) butter
50 g (2 oz) plain flour
salt
freshly ground black pepper
300 ml (½ pint) milk
2 eggs, separated
25 g (1 oz) fresh white breadcrumbs
100 g (4 oz) blue cheese, finely diced
sticks of celery heart, to garnish

Preparation time: 25-30 minutes
Cooking time: 15 minutes
Oven: 220°C, 425°F, Gas Mark 7

The blue cheese can be Stilton, Danish Blue, Mycella, Dolcelatte or Roquefort. Use salt sparingly as these cheeses can be quite salty.

1. Melt the butter in a saucepan and stir in the flour, salt and pepper. Cook for 1 minute, then add the milk and cook, stirring, until thickened and smooth.
2. Allow to cool slightly, then beat in the egg yolks. Stir in the breadcrumbs and cheese until the cheese has melted.
3. Whisk the egg whites until stiff and fold into the mixture with a metal spoon.
To Freeze: Spoon into 6 buttered freezerproof ramekin dishes. Cover and freeze.
To Serve: Stand the dishes on a baking sheet and place in a preheated oven. Bake for 25-30 minutes or until risen, golden and set. Serve immediately with the celery sticks.

POTTED CHICKEN

225 g (8 oz) cooked chicken meat, finely minced
50 g (2 oz) cooked lean bacon or ham, finely minced
1 teaspoon grated lemon rind
2 teaspoons chopped parsley
¼ teaspoon dried tarragon
salt
freshly ground black pepper
100 g (4 oz) butter, melted
To garnish:
lettuce leaves
slices of tomato
sprigs of fresh parsley or tarragon

Preparation time: 10 minutes, plus chilling

1. Mix together the chicken, bacon or ham, lemon rind, herbs, salt and pepper with 50 g (2 oz) of the butter.
2. Press into individual freezerproof dishes or foil-lined patty tins.
3. Pour the remaining butter over the top of each. Leave to chill until the butter is set.
To Freeze: Wrap and freeze.
To Serve: Allow to thaw in the refrigerator for about 6 hours. If frozen in foil-lined patty tins, turn out on to plates lined with lettuce leaves. Serve garnished with a slice of tomato topped with a sprig of parsley or tarragon. Accompany with Melba toast.

Variation:
Potted Shrimps: Replace the chicken and ham with 225 g (8 oz) cooked peeled shrimps or prawns. Omit the tarragon and add a pinch of cayenne. Serve with lemon wedges instead of tomato slices.

FROM THE LEFT: Blue cheese soufflés; Potted chicken; Little pots of pâté

FRESH MACKEREL PÂTÉ

Serves 6
450 g (1 lb) fresh mackerel, cleaned and head removed
2 tablespoons lemon juice
1 medium onion, peeled and chopped
1 bay leaf
salt
freshly ground black pepper
1 tablespoon wine vinegar
2 teaspoons powdered gelatine
150 ml (¼ pint) soured cream
2 tablespoons chopped fresh coriander
To garnish:
shredded lettuce
cucumber slices

Preparation time: 25 minutes, plus cooling and chilling
Cooking time: 15 minutes

Fresh coriander has a distinctive, unusual flavour. If it is not available, use parsley and add 1 tablespoon creamed horseradish sauce.

1. Put the mackerel in a pan with the lemon juice, onion, bay leaf, salt and pepper.
2. Add enough water to cover, bring to the boil and simmer for 15 minutes. Cool in the water.
3. Lift out the mackerel, strain the liquid and reserve 6 tablespoons, together with the onion.
4. Remove all the skin and bones from the fish and put the flesh, with the onion, into an electric blender. Add the wine vinegar and 4 tablespoons of the reserved cooking liquid.
5. Sprinkle the gelatine on the remaining cooking liquid in a cup and leave to soak for 5 minutes, then stand the cup in a pan of simmering water and stir until the gelatine has completely dissolved.
6. Add to the blender with the cream and coriander. Process until smooth. Taste and adjust the seasoning.
To Freeze: Put into a 600 ml (1 pint) freezerproof fish mould or foil container. Allow to set. Cover and freeze.
To Serve: Allow to thaw in the refrigerator for 6-8 hours. Turn out and serve on a bed of shredded lettuce, garnished with quartered slices of cucumber. Serve with brown bread and butter.

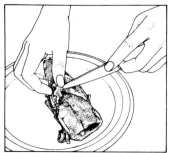

Carefully removing the skin.

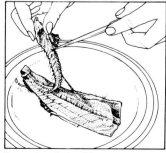

Removing the back bone.

SMOKED SALMON BOATS

Makes 8
75 g (3 oz) plain flour
pinch of salt
40 g (1½ oz) lard
2 tablespoons cold water
Filling:
75 g (3 oz) smoked salmon trimmings, finely chopped
1 tablespoon lemon juice
¼ teaspoon dried dill weed
1 tablespoon mayonnaise
3 tablespoons double cream, lightly whipped
salt
fresh ground black pepper
To garnish:
paprika
sprigs of fresh dill

Preparation time: 20 minutes
Cooking time: 15 minutes
Oven: 200°C, 400°F, Gas Mark 6

1. To make the pastry, sift the flour and salt into a bowl and rub in the lard until the mixture resembles fine breadcrumbs. Add the water and mix to a firm dough.
2. Roll out the dough and use to line 8 boat-shaped patty tins (barquette tins). Prick well and place on a baking sheet. Put into a preheated oven and bake for 15 minutes or until lightly coloured. Leave to cool in the tins for 10 minutes, then turn out onto a wire tray and allow to cool completely.
3. To make the filling, stir together all the ingredients and add salt and pepper to taste.
To Freeze: Put the filling into a rigid freezer container, cover and freeze. Pack the pastry boats separately in a rigid freezer container and freeze.
To Serve: Allow the filling to thaw in the refrigerator for about 6 hours. Thaw the pastry boats at room temperature for 30 minutes. Stir the filling, then spoon into the pastry boats. Sprinkle with paprika and serve garnished with fresh dill.

To line the boat-shaped patty tins, arrange them close together on a baking sheet. Roll out the pastry to 5 mm/¼ inch thick and large enough to cover them all. Lift the pastry on to a rolling pin and unroll over the boats. Press the pastry lightly into the tins, then run the rolling pin over the top to trim off the excess pastry. Mould each boat into shape, easing the pastry about 3 mm/⅛ inch above the edge of the tins, to allow for shrinkage during cooking. Prick the pastry thoroughly with a fork.

FROM THE LEFT: Gazpacho ice; Smoked salmon boats

GAZPACHO ICE

Serves 4-6
225 g (8 oz) tomatoes, chopped
50 g (2 oz) cucumber, chopped
50 g (2 oz) green pepper, cored, seeded and chopped
1 clove garlic, peeled and crushed
1 tablespoon wine vinegar
1 teaspoon paprika
2 tablespoons water
2 teaspoons powdered gelatine
100 g (4 oz) low fat soft cheese
150 ml (¼ pint) double cream
salt
freshly ground black pepper
few drops of edible red food colouring (optional)
To garnish:
lettuce leaves
8 pimento-stuffed green olives, chopped
sprig of watercress

Preparation time: 15 minutes, plus freezing

1. Put the tomatoes, cucumber, green pepper, garlic, vinegar and paprika into an electric blender and process until smooth. Rub the purée through a sieve.
2. Put the water in a cup, sprinkle over the gelatine and leave to soak for 5 minutes. Stand the cup in a pan of simmering water and stir until the gelatine is completely dissolved.
3. Gently whisk the cheese, cream and vegetable purée together until smooth and well combined. Whisk in the gelatine. Add salt, pepper and 1-2 drops of red colouring, (if using).
To Freeze: Pour into a rigid freezer container, cover and freeze for about 4 hours.
To Serve: Allow to soften in the refrigerator for 1 hour before serving. Spoon on to plates lined with lettuce leaves and top with the chopped olives and watercress.

LIGHT MEALS AND SNACKS

STUFFED PEPPERS

4 large green peppers
75 g (3 oz) long-grain rice
salt
1 large onion, peeled and chopped
1 tablespoon oil
100 g (4 oz) button mushrooms, sliced
25 g (1 oz) salted cashew nuts, chopped
50 g (2 oz) dried apricots, soaked overnight, drained and
    chopped
1 egg, beaten
a little Worcestershire sauce
freshly ground black pepper
Sauce:
25 g (1 oz) butter
25 g (1 oz) plain flour
300 ml (½ pint) milk
150 g (5 oz) Cotswold cheese, grated
1 teaspoon French mustard

Preparation time: 40 minutes
Cooking time: 1-1¼ hours
Oven: 180°C, 350°F, Gas Mark 4

1. Cut off the stalk end of each pepper. Scoop out the seeds. If the peppers do not stand straight, level the bases.
2. Cook the rice in boiling salted water until tender, about 10-12 minutes. Drain and rinse with hot water.
3. Gently fry the onion in the oil for about 5 minutes.
4. Add the mushrooms, nuts and apricots and cook for 3 minutes. Stir in the rice, egg, Worcestershire sauce, salt and pepper.
5. Fill the peppers with the rice mixture and stand them upright in an ovenproof dish.
6. Melt the butter in a saucepan, add the flour and cook for 1 minute, then gradually stir in the milk. Bring to the boil, stirring, and cook until smooth and thickened. Add the salt and pepper, half the cheese and the mustard. Pour the sauce round the peppers. Sprinkle with the remaining cheese. Cool.
To Freeze: Cover and freeze.
To Serve: Allow to thaw at room temperature for 3-4 hours. Replace cover with foil and cook in a preheated oven for about 1 hour, or until browned and tender.

Variation:
Fill the peppers with freshly made Savoury Mince (page 28). Pipe mashed potato on top, and pour round a tomato sauce. Freeze and cook as above.

OMELETTE PIZZA

2 tablespoons oil
1 small onion, finely chopped
225 g (8 oz) potatoes, peeled, parboiled and diced
½ green pepper, cored, seeded and diced
1 large tomato, skinned, seeded and chopped
6 pimento-stuffed green olives, chopped
6 eggs, beaten
salt
freshly ground black pepper
To serve:
1 tablespoon oil
15 g (½ oz) butter
75 g (3 oz) mature Cheddar cheese, grated
4 anchovy fillets, halved lengthways
4 pimento-stuffed green olives, halved

Preparation time: 20 minutes
Cooking time: 25 minutes

Spanish Omelette is full of interesting vegetables and flavours and makes a super snack. Here it is used as the base for a pizza topping which transforms it into more of a meal. Try the omelette on its own, cold, cut into small wedges as a cocktail savory with drinks.

1. Heat the oil in a 23 cm (9 inch) non-stick frying pan. Add the onion and fry gently until softened but not coloured. Add the potatoes, green pepper, tomato and olives and cook, stirring gently, for 5 minutes.
2. Beat the eggs with the salt and pepper and pour into the pan. Let the mixture run through the vegetables, then cook for about 5 minutes or until set underneath.
3. Put the pan under a preheated medium hot grill and cook until the top is set and very slightly coloured. Loosen the omelette with a spatula, shaking the pan, and turn out on to a sheet of greaseproof paper on top of a sheet of foil. Cool.
To Freeze: Wrap in the greaseproof paper and foil and freeze.
To Serve: Allow to thaw in the refrigerator for 4-6 hours. Heat the oil and butter in the frying pan. Place the omelette in the pan and reheat gently for 15 minutes, shaking the pan occasionally. Top with the cheese, then put under a preheated hot grill to melt. Garnish with the anchovy strips and olives, and serve immediately with hot garlic bread and salad.

Stuffed peppers; Omelette pizza

SANDWICHES

Many wives and mothers are making packed lunches every day for their husbands and children. Sandwiches are most convenient for packing and eating, but they take time to make and need to be really fresh. Freezer sandwiches are ideal. They can be made at any time, frozen interleaved, uncut or cut ready as you prefer. Take them out of the freezer early in the morning, wrap and pack, and they will be just thawed and very fresh by lunchtime. If you prefer, freeze the fillings, using up odds and ends, and then make up the sandwiches on the day they are required.

Most of the traditional and favourite fillings can be used; just beware of hard-boiled egg. It must be very well mashed with salad cream or a yogurt mayonnaise – whole slices of egg go very rubbery with freezing.

Here are two rather unusual fillings.

CURRIED BEEF AND BANANA SANDWICHES

Makes 10 rounds
350 g (12 oz) corned beef, mashed
1½ teaspoons curry paste
150 ml (¼ pint) banana yogurt
salt
butter, for spreading
20 slices of white bread

1. Mix together the corned beef, curry paste, yogurt and salt to taste. Butter the bread.
2. Spread the filling over half the slices of bread and top with the remaining slices.

SMOKED FISH SANDWICHES

Makes 10 rounds
350 g (12 oz) kipper fillets, cooked, skinned and minced
grated rind and juice of 1 lemon
1 small dessert apple, peeled, cored and minced
salt
freshly ground black pepper
butter, for spreading
20 slices of brown bread
mayonnaise

1. Mix together the kipper, lemon rind and juice and apple and season to taste with salt and pepper.
2. Lightly butter the bread, spread half the slices of brown bread with mayonnaise, then the filling. Top with the remaining bread.
3. Serve chilled, cut into fingers.

FAMILY SANDWICH

Serves 4-6
1 x 18 cm (7 inch) round granary or wholemeal loaf
softened butter
Egg filling:
3 eggs, beaten
2 tablespoons milk
15 g (½ oz) butter
salt
freshly ground black pepper
3 spring onions, finely chopped
Chicken filling:
175 g (6 oz) cooked chicken meat, minced
1 stick celery, thinly sliced
2-3 tablespoons mayonnaise
1 teaspoon curry paste
Cheese filling:
175 g (6 oz) Cheddar cheese, finely grated
2 tomatoes, skinned and chopped
To serve:
mustard and cress
cucumber slices
green pepper rings
radishes
watercress

Preparation time: 20 minutes

This is a good way of using up any leftovers of meat or cheese, salad ingredients, etc. The loaf can be taken on a picnic or eaten for a light lunch or supper at home. The fillings can be varied according to what you find in the fridge!

1. Put the eggs into a saucepan with the milk, butter and salt and pepper. Cook over a gentle heat, stirring, until scrambled. Add the spring onions and leave to cool.
2. Mix together the chicken and celery. Add enough mayonnaise to make a spreading consistency and stir in curry paste to taste.
3. Mix together the cheese and tomato.
4. Cut the loaf into 4 horizontally to make layers like a cake. Spread each cut surface with butter. Spread 1 layer with each filling and reassemble the loaf.
To Freeze: Wrap in foil and freeze.
To Serve: Allow to thaw in the refrigerator for 6 hours or overnight. Unwrap, slice vertically and serve with mixed salad ingredients.

FROM THE LEFT: Family sandwich; Lamb pitta pockets

LAMB PITTA POCKETS

Marinade:

2 tablespoons oil
2 tablespoons red wine
¼ teaspoon chilli powder
¼ teaspoon ground coriander
1 bouquet garni
salt
freshly ground black pepper
350 g (12 oz) neck fillet of lamb, cut in thin slices
1 medium onion, peeled and thinly sliced
2 teaspoons sesame seeds
4 pitta breads
4 teaspoons mint jelly

To serve:

shredded Chinese leaves or lettuce
tomato slices
slices pickled cucumber

Preparation time: 20 minutes, plus marinating
Cooking time: 50-60 minutes
Oven: 190°C, 375°F, Gas Mark 5

Make your own 'take-away' kebabs – a good standby for supper, or for a barbecue party. You can vary the seasoning in the marinade to suit your taste.

1. To make the marinade mix together all the ingredients in a bowl, with salt and pepper to taste. Add the lamb, onion and sesame seeds and stir well. Leave to marinate for 4 hours or overnight, turning and stirring occasionally.
2. Transfer the lamb mixture to a saucepan and cook gently for 25-30 minutes or until the lamb and onions are tender. Discard the bouquet garni.
3. Cut the pitta breads nearly in half to make a pocket. Spread the mint jelly inside the pockets. Fill with the cooked meat mixture. Cool.
To Freeze: Wrap each pitta in freezer foil, seal and freeze.
To Serve: Put the frozen pitta parcels on a baking sheet and place in a preheated oven. Cook for 25-30 minutes or until hot through. Remove the foil, wrap in a paper serviette, and add Chinese leaves or lettuce, tomato and cucumber to each. Serve warm.

HOMEMADE BAPS

Makes 8
150 ml (¼ pint) milk
150 ml (¼ pint) water
1 teaspoon sugar
2 teaspoons dried yeast
450 g (1 lb) strong plain white bread flour
2 teaspoons salt
50 g (2 oz) lard

Preparation time: 35 minutes, plus proving
Cooking time: 10-15 minutes
Oven: 220°C, 425°F, Gas Mark 7

This recipe can also be used to make 12 smaller rolls or a loaf in a 450 g (1 lb) loaf tin. The cooking time for the rolls is the same, cook the loaf for 25 minutes. Homemade baps can be served warm for breakfast or used for packed lunches, filled with meat or cheese and salad.

1. Place the milk and water in a saucepan and warm to a comfortable finger-hot temperature.
2. Pour into a bowl, stir in the sugar and sprinkle the yeast on top. Leave until risen and frothy, about 10 minutes.
3. Sift the flour and salt into a bowl. Rub in the lard until the mixture resembles breadcrumbs. Stir in the yeast liquid and mix to a soft dough which cleanly comes away from the sides of the bowl.
4. Knead on a floured board until smooth and elastic, about 5 minutes. Put into a lightly floured bowl, cover with oiled cling film and leave to rise in a warm place for 1-1½ hours or until doubled in bulk.
5. Turn out on to the floured board and knead lightly. Divide into 8 equal pieces and knead each to form a smooth round with the gathers underneath. Roll or flatten each round with the palm of the hand to about 10 cm (4 inches) in diameter.
6. Place on a floured baking sheet and cover with a sheet of oiled cling film. Leave to prove in a warm place for about 20 minutes, or until risen.
7. Remove the cling film and dust the baps with a little flour. Bake in a preheated oven for about 10 minutes or until lightly coloured. Transfer immediately to a wire rack and cover with a clean tea towel. This softens the tops, giving the characteristic texture of baps. Leave to cool.
To Freeze: Pack in freezer bags, seal and freeze.
To Serve: Allow to thaw at room temperature for about 1 hour, or warm in a preheated oven (180°C, 350°F, Gas Mark 4) for about 10 minutes, wrapped in foil to keep the baps soft.

Variation:
Quick Supper Baps: Cut the baps in half, toast lightly and spread with a little butter. Cover with slices of tomato, thinly sliced garlic or smoked sausage and top with grated Cheddar cheese. Grill for about 5 minutes until the cheese is melted and browned. Serve hot.

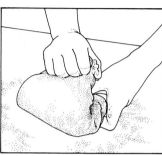
Stir in the yeast liquid until the dough leaves the sides of the bowl

Knead the dough on a floured board. Fold the dough in half

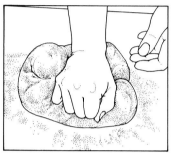
Push the dough away with the heel of your hand and fold in half again

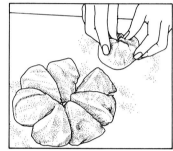
Cut into equal portions, then knead into smooth rounds

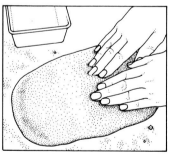
With your fingertips, press out the wholemeal dough to form an oblong

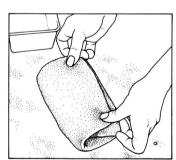
Fold the dough into 3 to fit the shape of the tin

WHOLEMEAL BREAD

Makes 2 x 1 kg (2 lb) and 2 x 450 g (1 lb) loaves

1 litre (1¾ pints) hand-hot water
1 tablespoon malt extract
1 tablespoon dried yeast
1.5 kg (3¼ lb) wholemeal flour
2 tablespoons salt
50 g (2 oz) lard
lard for greasing
sesame or poppy seeds

Preparation time: 30 minutes, plus proving
Cooking time: 40 minutes
Oven: 220°C, 425°F, Gas Mark 7

If liked, you can vary the flour, using granary or wheat-meal in place of the wholemeal. Malt extract can be found in the homebrew beer and wine section of big chemists.

1. Put 300 ml (½ pint) of the warm water into a bowl. Stir in the malt until nearly dissolved and sprinkle the yeast on top. Leave until frothy, about 10 minutes.
2. Put the flour and salt into a large bowl. Rub in the lard until the mixture resembles breadcrumbs.
3. Add the yeast liquid and the rest of the warm water and mix until the dough leaves the sides of the bowl.
4. Turn on to a floured board (use any plain white flour for this) and knead until the dough is smooth and elastic, about 10 minutes.
5. Divide the dough into 4 portions, 2 weighing 1 kg (2 lb) and two 450 g (1 lb). They may not weigh quite the full amount, but it does not matter.
6. Knead each portion, then press or roll out to an oblong as wide as the long side of the tin, and as long as 3 times the short side of the tin. Fold into 3 and turn over so the joins are underneath. Grease two 1 kg (2 lb) loaf tins and two 450 g (1 lb) loaf tins with lard and put in the shaped dough.
7. Cover with oiled cling film, or put each tin into a large polythene bag. Leave to prove in a warm place for 1-1½ hours or until risen to the tops of the tins.
8. Brush the top of each loaf lightly with water and sprinkle with sesame or poppy seeds.
9. Bake in a preheated oven for about 40 minutes or until browned and hollow-sounding when tapped on the bottom.
10. Turn out and cool on a wire tray.
To Freeze: Wrap in foil and freeze. One loaf can be sliced ready for toasting.
To Serve: Allow to thaw at room temperature for 2-3 hours. For toast, take frozen slices and put straight under the grill or into the toaster.

Wholemeal bread; Homemade baps; Quick supper baps

CHICKEN OR TURKEY CHOWDER

100 g (4 oz) bacon, rinded and finely chopped
1 onion, peeled and finely chopped
2 sticks celery, sliced
225 g (8 oz) potatoes, peeled and diced
100 g (4 oz) sweetcorn kernels
450 ml (¾ pint) chicken stock
225 g (8 oz) cooked chicken or turkey meat, diced
salt
freshly ground black pepper
pinch of ground mace
150 ml (¼ pint) half cream, to serve

Preparation time: 15 minutes
Cooking time: 20 minutes

Chowder is an American word which is thought to come from the name of the cooking pot that the fishermen used to throw their catch into when they returned safely from sea. The community used to share in celebrating their homecoming. The thick soup/stew was particularly a feature of New England cooking. Today, many ingredients other than fish are used to make chowder.

1. Fry the bacon gently in a saucepan until the fat runs. Add the onion and fry for 5 minutes or until softened.
2. Add the celery, potatoes, sweetcorn and stock. Bring to the boil, then cover and simmer for 15 minutes.
3. Add the chicken or turkey and cook for a further 5 minutes. Add the salt and pepper, and mace. Remove from the heat and cool.
To Freeze: Put into a rigid freezer container, cover and freeze.
To Serve: Allow to thaw at room temperature for 3-4 hours. Place in a saucepan and slowly bring to the boil, stirring occasionally. Simmer for 5 minutes. Stir in the cream, taste and adjust the seasoning and serve with warmed Soda Bread (page 11) and butter.

FROM THE LEFT: Sunday night soup; Chicken or turkey chowder; Pancakes Arnold Bennett

PANCAKES ARNOLD BENNETT

100 g (4 oz) plain flour
¼ teaspoon salt
1 egg
300 ml (½ pint) milk
lard for frying
3 tablespoons single cream, to serve
Filling:
225 g (8 oz) smoked cod or haddock fillet
150 ml (¼ pint) milk
150 ml (¼ pint) water
25 g (1 oz) hard margarine
25 g (1 oz) plain flour
salt
freshly ground black pepper
pinch of grated nutmeg
2 hard-boiled eggs, chopped

Preparation time: 45 minutes
Cooking time: 30 minutes
Oven: 200°C, 400°F, Gas Mark 6

This is a perfect freezer dish. The pancakes can be frozen, interleaved, ready for thawing and filling, or they can be filled and frozen as a complete dish. To have pancakes in the freezer is to have a meal ready in minutes.

1. Sift the flour and salt into a bowl. Add the egg and half the milk and whisk to a smooth batter, then stir in the rest of the milk.
2. Melt a little lard in an 18 cm (7 inch) frying pan over medium heat. Pour in enough batter just to cover the bottom of the pan. Cook until the underside of the pancake is browned.

3. Turn the pancake and cook the other side. Lift out on to a sheet of foil or a plate. Make seven more pancakes, and stack them, interleaved with a strip of greaseproof paper. If freezing them unfilled, cool, wrap in freezer foil and freeze.
4. To make the filling, put the fish into a saucepan with the milk and water. Bring to the boil, then cover and simmer for 10 minutes. Drain the fish, reserving the liquid. Remove all skin and bones and flake the fish.
5. Bring the reserved liquid to the boil. Mix the margarine and flour to a smooth paste. Add to the liquid in small pieces and whisk until smooth and thickened.
6. Season with salt and pepper. Add the nutmeg, and stir in the fish and chopped eggs. Divide the filling between the pancakes and roll up.
To Freeze: Put the pancakes into a rigid freezer container. Cover and freeze.
To Serve: Allow to thaw at room temperature for 3-4 hours. If the container is not ovenproof, transfer the pancakes to a baking dish and cover. Cook in a preheated oven for 30 minutes, or until hot. Trickle the cream over the top just before serving.

Variation:
Spicy Meat Pancakes: Take 350 g (12 oz) freshly prepared Savoury Mince (page 28) and add 2 tablespoons tomato purée, 1 tablespoon Worcestershire sauce, 1 garlic clove, peeled and crushed, 1 teaspoon ground cumin and 1 tablespoon sweet pickle. Heat all the ingredients together in a saucepan and use to fill the pancakes. Freeze as above. Thaw, then top with 3 tablespoons plain unsweetened yogurt and sprinkle with Parmesan cheese. Reheat as above.

SUNDAY NIGHT SOUP

Serves 8
750 g (1½ lb) smoked ham knuckle joint
175 g (6 oz) dried peas
50 g (2 oz) yellow lentils
1 large onion, peeled and chopped
2 bay leaves
freshly ground black pepper
1.75 litres (3 pints) water

Preparation time: 10 minutes, plus soaking
Cooking time: 2 hours

This is a substantial soup and can be served as a main meal with its chunky pieces of ham.

1. Put the knuckle, peas and lentils in a large saucepan, cover with cold water and leave to soak for 12 hours.
2. Drain off the water. Add the onion, bay leaves, pepper and the measured water, which should just cover the ingredients.
3. Bring to the boil, then cover and simmer for about 2 hours or until the peas are tender.
4. Lift out the knuckle. Remove the skin and bone and discard. Cut the meat into chunks and reserve.
5. Put the soup into a blender and process to a very smooth consistency. This may have to be done twice. Add the ham to the purée. Cool completely.
To Freeze: Pack into rigid freezer containers, cover and freeze.
To Serve: Allow to thaw at room temperature for 4-5 hours. Place in a saucepan and slowly bring to the boil, stirring occasionally. Taste and adjust the seasoning, and add a little milk if the soup is too thick. Serve with brown rolls or toast.

SPAGHETTI LAYER BAKE

2 tablespoons oil
1 large onion, peeled and chopped
450 g (1 lb) tomatoes, skinned and chopped
100 g (4 oz) mushrooms, chopped
1 tablespoon tomato purée
1 teaspoon dried oregano
salt
freshly ground black pepper
225 g (8 oz) minced pork
1 garlic clove, peeled and crushed
175 g (6 oz) long spaghetti
Topping:
25 g (1 oz) butter
2 tablespoons plain flour
300 ml (½ pint) milk
1 egg, beaten
1 teaspoon dry mustard
75 g (3 oz) mature Cheddar cheese, grated

Preparation time: 1 hour
Cooking time: 1-1¼ hours
Oven: 190°C, 375°F, Gas Mark 5

1. Heat 1 tablespoon of the oil in a saucepan. Add the onion and fry until soft but not coloured. Add the tomatoes, mushrooms, tomato purée, oregano and salt and pepper. Cook for 5 minutes.
2. To make meatballs, mix together the pork, garlic, salt and pepper. With floured hands, shape the mixture into 16 balls.
3. Heat the rest of the oil in a frying pan. Add the pork balls and fry until sealed and lightly browned on all sides. As the pork balls brown, remove them from the pan and drain on paper towels.
4. Bring a large saucepan of salted water to the boil. Add the spaghetti, bring the water back to the boil and simmer for about 8 minutes or until just 'al dente'. Drain well and add to the tomato and mushroom sauce.
5. Place half the spaghetti mixture into a 1.75 litre (3 pint) deep freezerproof dish. Add all the meatballs, then cover with the rest of the spaghetti.
6. To make the topping, melt the butter in a saucepan. Add the flour and cook for 1 minute. Gradually stir in the milk. Bring to the boil, stirring continuously, and cook until thickened and smooth. Remove from the heat and allow to cool slightly. Add the egg, mustard and cheese and stir until well blended. Add salt and pepper.
7. Pour the sauce over the top of the spaghetti to cover it completely. Allow to cool.
To Freeze: Cover and freeze.
To Serve: Allow to thaw at room temperature for 3-4 hours. Remove the cover, and cook in a preheated oven for 1-1¼ hours or until hot and bubbling and the topping has set and browned. Serve with a green salad or vegetables.

CANNELLONI WITH TOMATO SAUCE

Sauce:
2 x 400 g (14 oz) cans chopped tomatoes
1 onion, peeled and finely chopped
2 tablespoons tomato purée
1 teaspoon dried mixed herbs
1 red pepper, cored, seeded and finely diced
150 ml (¼ pint) red wine
150 ml (¼ pint) chicken stock
2 teaspoons redcurrant jelly
salt
freshly ground black pepper
Filling:
500 g (1 lb) fresh spinach, rinsed, cooked, drained and finely chopped
100 g (4 oz) cottage cheese with chives
1 tablespoon semolina or ground rice
¼ teaspoon grated nutmeg
8 cannelloni tubes
grated Parmesan cheese, to serve

Preparation time: 30 minutes
Cooking time: 20 minutes
Oven: 190°C, 375°F, Gas Mark 5

Filling cooked cannelloni tubes can be quite difficult. In this recipe, the pasta is filled without being pre-cooked. The sauce is made thinner than usual, the extra liquid is absorbed by the pasta during cooking. If you prefer, the pasta can be pre-cooked, following the directions on the packet. Use slightly less liquid for the sauce.

1. To make the sauce, place all the ingredients into a saucepan. Bring to the boil, then cover and simmer for 20 minutes, stirring occasionally.
2. Meanwhile, mix together the filling ingredients and spoon into the cannelloni tubes.
3. Spread half the sauce in a rigid freezer container or shallow ovenproof dish. Arrange the stuffed cannelloni in a single layer in the container, making sure they are not touching and that there is sauce under and between them.
4. Cover completely with the rest of the sauce. Allow the sauce to cool.
To Freeze: Cover with freezer film and foil or a lid and freeze.
To Serve: If using freezer film, remove it but leave the foil, or lid. Cook from frozen in a preheated oven for 1¼ hours or until heated through and the tubes are tender. Sprinkle with the Parmesan cheese and serve, with extra cheese in a separate dish.

FROM THE LEFT: Spaghetti layer bake; Steamed meat loaf

STEAMED MEAT LOAF

225 g (8 oz) leftover roast beef or lamb
100 g (4 oz) cooked shoulder ham or bacon joint
1 small onion, peeled
4 parsley sprigs
75 g (3 oz) fresh breadcrumbs
1 egg
1 teaspoon Worcestershire sauce
1 teaspoon salt
freshly ground black pepper

Preparation time: 10 minutes
Cooking time: 2 hours

This meat loaf is just as delicious cold, in sandwiches or with salad. Serve it hot, with ratatouille and baked jacket potatoes.

1. Mince the meat, ham or bacon, onion and parsley. Mix with the rest of the ingredients.
2. Pack into a greased 450 g (1 lb) pudding basin. Cover with buttered greaseproof paper and foil and seal well.
3. Place the basin in a saucepan of boiling water and steam for 2 hours. Cool.
To Freeze: If you wish, turn out of the basin, and wrap in cling film and freezer foil. Or leave in the basin, cover with fresh foil and freeze.
To Serve: Allow to thaw for about 6 hours in the refrigerator. Slice to serve cold. To serve warm, replace in the basin, cover and steam for 1 hour. Serve with vegetables.

HAM QUICHE

100 g (4 oz) plain flour
pinch of salt
25 g (1 oz) hard margarine
25 g (1 oz) lard
1-2 tablespoons water
Filling:
175 g (6 oz) cooked shoulder ham, minced
2 tablespoons chopped mixed fresh herbs
1 small onion, peeled and minced
1 large tomato, finely chopped
2 eggs, beaten
150 ml (¼ pint) milk

Preparation time: 20 minutes
Cooking time: 45-50 minutes
Oven: 190°C, 375°F, Gas Mark 5

This quiche can be served warm or cold, and is ideal for picnics. It can be made as a pie, using pastry made with 175 g (6 oz) flour and 40 g (1½ oz) of each fat.

1. Sift the flour and salt into a bowl. Rub in the fats until the mixture resembles breadcrumbs. Mix with water to a firm dough.
2. Roll out the dough and line an 18 cm (7 inch) flan ring placed on a baking sheet.
3. To make the filling, mix together all the ingredients and pour into the pastry case.
4. Bake in a preheated oven for about 45 minutes or until set and lightly coloured. Cool, then remove the flan ring.
To Freeze: Open freeze on the baking sheet, then wrap and return to the freezer.
To Serve: Allow to thaw at room temperature for 3-4 hours. Serve cold, or warm for 15 minutes in a preheated oven (180°C, 350°F, Gas Mark 4).

Ham quiche; Chicken and asparagus pasties

CHICKEN AND ASPARAGUS PASTIES

Makes 4
225 g (8 oz) self-raising flour
1 teaspoon salt
50 g (2 oz) lard
50 g (2 oz) hard margarine
3-4 tablespoons water
beaten egg, to glaze
Filling:
1 x 200 g (7 oz) can asparagus tips
milk
15 g (½ oz) butter
1 tablespoon plain flour
225 g (8 oz) cooked chicken meat, finely chopped
salt
freshly ground black pepper

Preparation time: 30 minutes
Cooking time: 15 minutes
Oven: 200°C, 400°F, Gas Mark 6

1. Sift the flour and salt into a bowl. Rub in the fats until the mixture resembles breadcrumbs. Mix with water to give a firm dough.
2. To make the filling, drain the asparagus, reserving the liquid. Make the liquid up to 150 ml (¼ pint) with milk. Chop the asparagus.
3. Melt the butter in a saucepan, stir in the flour and cook for 1 minute. Gradually stir in the liquid and bring to the boil, stirring continuously. Cook until thickened and smooth.
4. Add the chicken, asparagus, salt and pepper. Cool.
5. Roll out the dough and cut four 18 cm (7 inch) rounds, using a saucepan lid as a guide.
6. Divide the filling between the rounds. Dampen the edges, form into semi-circles, and seal well. Flute the edges or decorate with the prongs of a fork.
To Freeze: Open freeze on a baking sheet. When firm, wrap and pack in a freezer bag. Return to the freezer.
To Serve: Unwrap the pasties and place on a baking sheet. Brush with beaten egg and bake from frozen in a preheated oven for about 40 minutes or until golden brown. Serve warm.

Variation:
Cornish Pasties: Make the pastry as above. For the filling, combine: 1 onion, peeled and finely chopped; 225 g (8 oz) potato, peeled, par-boiled and diced; 100 g (4 oz) frying steak, finely diced; salt and freshly ground black pepper. Roll out the dough and cut into rounds as above. Top with the filling. Bring the edges of the dough to the top, dampen, seal well, and flute or twist. Glaze with beaten egg. Bake in a preheated oven (200°C, 400°F, Gas Mark 6) for 40 minutes. Cool and freeze as above. Serve cold, or reheated for 30 minutes from frozen in a preheated oven (180°C, 350°F, Gas Mark 4).

CHEESE AND ONION TARTS

100 g (4 oz) plain flour
pinch of salt
25 g (1 oz) hard margarine
25 g (1 oz) lard
1-2 tablespoons water
Filling:
15 g (½ oz) butter
1 medium onion, peeled and chopped
1 dessert apple, cored and grated
50 g (2 oz) mature Cheddar cheese, grated
1 egg
milk
salt
freshly ground black pepper

Preparation time: 25 minutes
Cooking time: 30-35 minutes
Oven: 190°C, 375°F, Gas Mark 5

Apple and cheese go so well together and are here combined in a savoury tart. The best apple flavour comes from Cox's Orange Pippins, one of the favourite English dessert apples.

1. Sift the flour and salt into a bowl. Rub in the fats until the mixture resembles breadcrumbs. Mix with water to a firm dough.
2. Divide the dough into 4 portions. Roll out and line four 10 cm (4 inch) tart tins or Yorkshire pudding tins.
3. Melt the butter in a small frying pan, add the onion and fry until softened and lightly coloured.
4. Divide the onion between the pastry cases and cover with the grated apple and cheese.
5. Beat the egg in a measuring jug and make up to 150 ml (¼ pint) with milk. Add salt and pepper and pour equally into the pastry cases.
6. Bake in a preheated oven for 30-35 minutes or until golden and set. Cool.
To Freeze: Pack in a freezer container, cover and freeze.
To Serve: Remove from the tins and allow to thaw at room temperature for 3 hours. Serve either cold, or warmed for 15 minutes in a preheated oven (180°C, 350°F, Gas Mark 4).

FRANKFURTER RICE WITH GHERKINS

25 g (1 oz) butter
1 tablespoon oil
1 large Spanish onion, peeled and chopped
175 g (6 oz) long-grain rice
300 ml (½ pint) chicken stock
50 g (2 oz) sweetcorn kernels
40 g (1½ oz) sultanas
225 g (8 oz) frankfurters, sliced
salt
freshly ground black pepper
To serve:
2 sweet/sour gherkins, chopped
1 hard-boiled egg, chopped

Preparation time: 15 minutes
Cooking time: 30-35 minutes
Oven: 190°C, 375°F, Gas Mark 5

1. Melt the butter and oil in a saucepan, add the onion and cook gently for 5 minutes until softened but not coloured.
2. Stir in the rice and stock and bring to the boil. Simmer gently for about 25 minutes or until the rice is tender and the stock has been absorbed. Stir occasionally.
3. Add the sweetcorn, sultanas and frankfurters, salt and pepper. Cool.
To Freeze: Pack in a rigid container, cover and freeze.
To Serve: Allow to thaw at room temperature for 3-4 hours. Put into an ovenproof dish, cover and reheat in a preheated oven (180°C, 350°F, Gas Mark 4) for 1 hour stirring occasionally, until heated through. Stir in the gherkins and sprinkle with the chopped egg. Serve with green or tomato salad.

SPANISH RICE

100 g (4 oz) long-grain rice
salt
freshly ground black pepper
2 tablespoons oil
1 large Spanish onion, peeled and sliced
225 g (8 oz) tomatoes, skinned and quartered
225 g (8 oz) roast beef, chopped
50 g (2 oz) mushrooms, chopped
2 tablespoons tomato purée
½ teaspoon dried oregano
50 g (2 oz) Cheddar cheese, grated

Preparation time: 25 minutes
Cooking time: 40 minutes
Oven: 190°C, 375°F, Gas Mark 5

SAVOURY MINCE

Serves 10
Makes about 1.25 kg (2½ lb) cooked mince
1.5 kg (3 lb) minced beef
1 tablespoon oil
2 large onions, peeled and chopped
3 tablespoons rolled oats
¼ teaspoon ground mixed spice
2 teaspoons salt
freshly ground black pepper
To serve:
150 ml (¼ pint) beef stock
chopped parsley

Preparation time: 10 minutes
Cooking time: 45 minutes

1. Heat a non-stick frying pan and fry the mince, without any added fat, until it is browned and crumbly and most of the liquid has evaporated. Stir frequently.
2. In a separate frying pan, heat the oil, add the onions and fry until lightly browned.
3. Mix the onions and remaining ingredients into the mince, with pepper to taste, and cook gently, stirring occasionally, for about 30 minutes. Cool.
To Freeze: Pack in 225 g (8 oz) or 450 g (1 lb) quantities in rigid freezer containers, cover and freeze.
To Serve: Use as a filling for *Spicy meat pancakes* (page 23) or *Stuffed peppers* (page 16). To serve on its own, allow 450 g (1 lb) mince to thaw at room temperature for 3 hours. Put into a saucepan, add the stock and bring to the boil, stirring occasionally. Simmer for 15 minutes, taste and adjust the seasoning and serve with a good sprinkling of chopped parsley.

This makes a filling, tasty supper. If you haven't any leftover roast beef, use any cooked meat or smoked sausage.

1. Cook the rice in boiling salted water for about 10 minutes or until just tender. Drain and rinse with hot water.
2. Heat the oil in a frying pan, add the onion and fry until lightly coloured. Stir in the tomatoes, beef and mushrooms and cook for a further 5 minutes.
3. Stir in the tomato purée, oregano, rice, salt and pepper. Cool.
To Freeze: Put into a rigid freezer container, cover and freeze.
To Serve: Allow to thaw at room temperature for about 3 hours. Put into an ovenproof dish, sprinkle the cheese on top and cook in a preheated oven for about 40 minutes or until heated through. Finish under the grill to brown the cheese. Serve with a green salad.

CHICKEN STIR-FRY

1 red pepper, cored, seeded and cut into strips
350 g (12 oz) cauliflower florets
2 sticks celery, cut into 5 mm (¼ inch) slices
6 spring onions, cut into 2 cm (¾ inch) lengths
225 g (8 oz) courgettes, cut into 5 mm (¼ inch) slices
25 g (1 oz) butter
1 tablespoon oil
4 chicken breasts, skinned, boned and cut into strips
100 g (4 oz) button mushrooms, halved
To serve:
25 g (1 oz) butter
1 tablespoon oil
1-2 teaspoons cornflour
2 teaspoons soy sauce
1 teaspoon caster sugar
¼ teaspoon dried thyme
salt
freshly ground black pepper

Preparation time: 35 minutes
Cooking time: 10-15 minutes

The secret of this dish is to keep the vegetables very crisp. It is a good opportunity for using up small amounts of raw vegetables, so you can vary the mixture accordingly.

1. Bring a saucepan of lightly salted water to the boil. Add the red pepper, cauliflower, celery, spring onions and courgettes and boil for 1 minute. Drain and cool in cold water. Drain again thoroughly. Spread out on a baking tray.
2. Heat the butter and oil in a frying pan. Add the chicken strips and fry gently for 5 minutes. Add the mushrooms and cook for 1 minute. Lift out the chicken and mushrooms with a slotted spoon and spread on the baking tray. Cool.
To Freeze: Open freeze on the baking tray. When solid, put into a freezer container and cover. Return to the freezer.
To Serve: Heat the butter and oil in a frying pan or wok, add the chicken and vegetables and stir-fry quickly for 5 minutes. Stir together with cornflour, soy sauce, sugar and thyme and add to the pan. Cook, stirring, until thickened. Add salt and pepper to taste, and serve with boiled rice or noodles.

FROM THE LEFT: Spanish rice; Chicken stir-fry

MAIN MEALS

OLD-FASHIONED CHICKEN PIE

Filling:
40 g (1½ oz) butter
40 g (1½ oz) plain flour
pinch of ground mace
salt
freshly ground black pepper
300 ml (½ pint) good chicken stock
150 ml (¼ pint) milk
1 small onion, peeled
2 bay leaves
350 g (12 oz) cooked chicken meat, cut into chunks
grated rind of ½ lemon
Pastry:
175 g (6 oz) plain flour
salt
40 g (1½ oz) lard
40 g (1½ oz) butter or hard margarine
beaten egg, to glaze

Preparation time: 40 minutes
Cooking time: 15 minutes
Oven: 200°C, 400°F, Gas Mark 6

1. Melt the butter in a saucepan. Add the flour, mace, salt and pepper and cook for 1 minute. Whisk in the stock and milk. Cook, stirring constantly, until smooth and thickened.
2. Add the onion and bay leaves. Remove from the heat, cover the surface of the sauce with a piece of cling film and set aside.
3. To make the pastry, sift the flour and salt into a bowl and rub in the fats until the mixture resembles crumbs. Add enough water to make a firm dough.
4. Take the onion and bay leaves out of the sauce and discard. Stir in the chicken and lemon rind. Pour the mixture into a 900 ml (1½ pint) freezer-proof pie dish with a pie funnel in the centre.
5. Roll out the dough and cut to fit the pie dish. Place on top. Seal the edges well, knock up and flute with a knife and decorate with the pastry trimmings cut into leaf shapes. Brush with beaten egg.
To Freeze: Open freeze. When solid, wrap in foil and return to the freezer.
To Serve: Unwrap the pie. Place on a baking sheet and bake from frozen in a preheated oven for about 1¼ hours or until the pastry is browned and the filling hot and bubbling. Cover with foil if the pastry browns too quickly. Serve with vegetables.

GOLDEN CHICKEN CASSEROLE

4 chicken quarters
4 tablespoons plain flour
salt
freshly ground black pepper
4 tablespoons oil
25 g (1 oz) butter
1 large onion, peeled, quartered and sliced
1 teaspoon turmeric
1 x 400 g (14 oz) can tomatoes
300 ml (½ pint) medium cider
100 g (4 oz) sweetcorn kernels
1 yellow pepper, cored, seeded and cut in rings
1 Golden Delicious apple, cored and sliced

Preparation time: 30 minutes
Cooking time: 40 minutes
Oven: 180°C, 350°F, Gas Mark 4

Turmeric has very little flavour but gives a glowing golden colour to this casserole. Yellow food colouring will do as a substitute. Yellow peppers can be found in many of the bigger supermarkets and greengrocers. If they are not available, use a red pepper.

1. Toss the chicken quarters in flour seasoned with salt and pepper to coat them thoroughly. Heat the oil in a frying pan, add the chicken and brown lightly on all sides. Remove to a 2.25 litre (4 pint) casserole.
2. Add the butter to the frying pan, then the onion and fry until lightly golden. Stir in any remaining seasoned flour with the turmeric and cook for 1 minute.
3. Drain the liquid from the tomatoes. Add the liquid to the frying pan with the cider. Cook until thickened, stirring constantly.
4. Cut the tomatoes into quarters. Add to the casserole with the sweetcorn and pepper rings. Pour over the cider sauce. Cover the casserole and cook in a preheated oven for about 40 minutes. Cool.
To Freeze: Pack into a rigid freezer container, cover and freeze.
To Serve: Allow to thaw at room temperature for 3-4 hours. Return to the casserole, cover and reheat in a preheated oven for about 30 minutes. Stir in the apple and cook for a further 15 minutes. Taste and adjust the seasoning. Serve with vegetables.

Old fashioned chicken pie; Golden chicken casserole

MRS B'S PIE

freshly made *Savoury mince*, made with 450 g (1 lb) minced
   beef (page 28)
4 carrots, peeled and grated
100 g (4 oz) frozen peas
2 celery sticks, sliced
2 tomatoes, sliced
750 g (1½ lb) potatoes, peeled and freshly cooked
25 g (1 oz) butter
2 tablespoons milk
salt
freshly ground black pepper
a little oil

Preparation time: 45 minutes
Cooking time: 1¼ hours
Oven: 190°C, 375°F, Gas Mark 5

1. Mix together the mince, carrots, peas and celery. Put into a 900 ml (1½ pint) freezerproof pie dish. Cover with the tomato slices.
2. Mash the potatoes with the butter and milk until light and fluffy. Season with salt and pepper and spread over the tomatoes. Roughen the top with a fork. Cool.
To Freeze: Cover with foil and freeze.
To Serve: Allow to thaw at room temperature for 3-4 hours. Uncover, brush the potato with a little oil and bake in a preheated oven for about 1¼ hours or until heated through and the potato is browned. Finish under the grill if necessary.

Variation:
Omit the carrots, peas and celery and add 1 x 225 g (8 oz) can baked beans in tomato sauce to the meat. Stir 50 g (2 oz) grated Cheddar cheese into the mashed potato and continue as above.

TURKEY NOODLE RING

225 g (8 oz) egg noodles
salt
1 tablespoon oil
75 g (3 oz) butter
Filling:
300 ml (½ pint) chicken stock
1 bay leaf
1 onion, peeled
4 cloves
40 g (1½ oz) butter
40 g (1½ oz) plain flour
150 ml (¼ pint) milk
salt
freshly ground black pepper
350 g (12 oz) cooked turkey meat, cubed
2 canned pimentos, drained and sliced
1 tablespoon chopped parsley
3 tablespoons single cream
finely chopped parsley, to garnish

Preparation time: 30 minutes
Cooking time: 30 minutes
Oven: 160°C, 325°F, Gas Mark 3

1. Cook the noodles in plenty of boiling salted water, with the oil added, for about 10 minutes or until just tender. Drain well and return to the pan. Add the butter and stir until it has melted. Pack the noodles into a freezerproof ring mould and cool.
2. Place the chicken stock in a saucepan with the bay leaf and the onion stuck with the cloves. Bring to the boil and simmer for about 10 minutes. Strain.
3. Melt the butter in a saucepan, stir in the flour and cook for 1 minute. Whisk in the flavoured stock and milk. Cook, stirring, until thickened and smooth. Add salt and pepper, the turkey, pimentos and parsley. Simmer for 5 minutes. Cool.
To Freeze: Pack the filling into a rigid freezer container and cover. Wrap the ring mould in foil. Freeze both.
To Serve: Allow to thaw at room temperature for 3-4 hours. Unwrap the ring mould and place in a roasting tin. Add enough water to the tin to come halfway up the sides of the mould and heat in a preheated oven for about 30 minutes or until heated through. Meanwhile, place the filling in a saucepan and bring slowly to the boil, stirring occasionally. Stir in the cream. Turn the noodle ring out on to a heated serving dish and put the filling into the centre. Sprinkle with the chopped parsley.

RABBIT AND BACON PUDDING

Pastry:
225 g (8 oz) self-raising flour
100 g (4 oz) shredded suet
salt
freshly ground white pepper
Filling:
225 g (8 oz) boneless rabbit, diced
100 g (4 oz) streaky bacon, rind removed, chopped
1 onion, peeled and finely chopped
50 g (2 oz) mushrooms, chopped
2 tomatoes, skinned and chopped
1 teaspoon dried sage
salt
freshly ground black pepper

Preparation time: 35 minutes
Cooking time: 2 hours

This warming pudding makes a change from the usual and traditional steak and kidney and is much cheaper. It can be frozen uncooked but a suet crust tastes better for the double cooking.

1. To make the pastry, sift the flour into a bowl and stir in the suet, salt and pepper. Add enough water to mix to a soft dough. Roll out three-quarters of the dough and use to line a buttered 1 kg (2 lb) pudding basin.
2. Fill the basin with layers of rabbit, bacon, onion, mushrooms and tomatoes, sprinkling the sage, salt and pepper in between each layer.
3. Roll out the remaining dough to make a lid. Place over the basin and press the edges to seal. Cover with buttered greaseproof paper and foil or a pudding cloth and seal over the edge of the basin.
4. Steam or boil for 2 hours, making sure that the water in the pan does not boil dry. Allow to cool.
To Freeze: Cover with fresh greaseproof paper and foil, then freeze.
To Serve: Allow to thaw in the refrigerator for 4-5 hours. Steam or boil for about 1 hour. Allow to stand for a couple of minutes so that the pastry shrinks slightly from the sides of the basin. Turn out and serve with green vegetables and a tomato or mushroom sauce.

Mrs B's pie; Turkey noodle ring

WINTER BEEF STEW

40 g (1½ oz) beef dripping
750 g (1½ lb) lean stewing beef, cut into 4 cm (1½ inch) cubes
2 onions, peeled and each cut into 8
2 carrots, peeled and sliced
1 parsnip, peeled and chopped
1 turnip, peeled and chopped
1 celery stick, sliced
2 tablespoons plain flour
1 x 225 g (8 oz) can tomatoes
½ teaspoon dried mixed herbs
1 teaspoon French mustard
450 ml (¾ pint) strong beef stock
salt
freshly ground black pepper
To serve:
2 tablespoons medium sherry
chopped parsley

Preparation time: 40 minutes
Cooking time: 2 hours

1. Heat the dripping in a heavy saucepan. Add the meat cubes, in batches, and fry until browned all over. Remove the meat cubes from the pan with a slotted spoon and drain well.
2. Add the vegetables to the pan and fry gently for 5 minutes.
3. Stir in the flour and cook gently for about 5 minutes or until the flour is golden brown.
4. Stir in the undrained tomatoes, herbs, mustard, stock, salt and pepper. Bring to the boil and stir until thickened and smooth.
5. Return the meat to the pan. Cover and simmer for about 1½ hours or until very tender, stirring occasionally. Cool.
To Freeze: Pack in a rigid container, cover and freeze.
To Serve: Allow to thaw at room temperature for 4-6 hours. Return to the pan and bring slowly to the boil, stirring occasionally. Add the sherry, and taste and adjust the seasoning. Serve sprinkled with parsley.

Variation:

Beef and Mushroom Crumble: Omit the carrots, parsnip, turnip and celery and substitute 225 g (8 oz) chopped mushrooms. Use only 150 ml (¼ pint) stock. When cooked, allow the stew to cool, then put it into an ovenproof freezer dish. Make a crumble topping by rubbing 75 g (3 oz) hard margarine into 175 g (6 oz) plain flour, seasoned with salt and pepper. Mix in 50 g (2 oz) grated cheese and sprinkle over the top of the stew.
To Freeze: Cover and freeze.
To Serve: Allow to thaw at room temperature for 4-6 hours. Uncover and bake in a preheated oven (190°C, 375°F, Gas Mark 5) for 50 minutes or until the crumble is golden brown.

SILVERSIDE CASSEROLE

Serves 6
1 kg (2 lb) joint of silverside of beef
2 beef stock cubes
900 ml (1½ pints) boiling water
2 bay leaves
6 black peppercorns
3 cloves
6 thin carrots, scraped and halved
12 small onions, peeled
225 g (8 oz) Jerusalem artichokes, peeled
Sauce:
150 ml (¼ pint) milk
25 g (1 oz) plain flour
25 g (1 oz) butter
salt
freshly ground black pepper
pinch of ground mace

Preparation time: 35 minutes
Cooking time: 1½ hours
Oven: 180°C, 350°F, Gas Mark 4

1. Put the joint of beef into a large deep saucepan. Dissolve the stock cubes in the water and pour over the beef. Add the spices tied in muslin. Bring to the boil and simmer for 1¼ hours. Skim.
2. Add the vegetables and cook a further 15 minutes. Lift out the meat and vegetables and cool. Strain the stock. Measure 150 ml (¼ pint) of the stock for the sauce.
3. To make the sauce, put the measured stock and milk in a saucepan and bring to the boil. Blend the flour and butter to a smooth paste. Whisk the paste into the hot liquid, in small pieces, until smooth and thickened. Add the salt and pepper and the mace. Cool.
4. Cut the joint into thick slices.
To Freeze: Lay the beef slices, overlapping, in an oven-proof freezer container, with the vegetables alongside. Pour over enough stock just to cover (freeze the rest separately for soup). Cover. Pack the sauce in a separate rigid container and cover. Freeze both.
To Serve: Allow to thaw at room temperature for 3-4 hours. Reheat the meat and vegetables, covered, in a preheated oven for about 45 minutes or until heated through. Meanwhile, place the sauce in a saucepan and bring slowly to the boil, stirring occasionally. Arrange the meat on a heated serving dish. Drain the vegetables, arrange down the centre, and pour over the sauce. Serve the stock from the meat dish separately.

FROM THE LEFT: Spiced brisket; Silverside casserole

SPICED BRISKET

Serves 6

1 kg (2 lb) boned joint of brisket of beef, rolled
1 x 290 g (10½ oz) can condensed beef consommé
1 small onion, peeled and sliced
6 strips of lemon rind
1 bay leaf
15 g (½ oz) pickling spice
salt
freshly ground black pepper
few parsley stalks

Preparation time: 20 minutes
Cooking time: 2-2½ hours
Oven: 150°C, 300°F, Gas Mark 2

1. Put the joint into a deep casserole. Pour over the consommé plus 1 can of water.
2. Add the onion, lemon rind and bay leaf. Tie the spice in muslin and add. Add salt and pepper together with the parsley stalks.
3. Cover and cook in a preheated oven for about 2 hours or until the meat is very tender.
4. Carefully lift out the joint and put it into a bowl or dish that will hold it snugly. Cover with a saucer and put a heavy weight on top. Leave to become quite cold, overnight.
5. Strain the liquid, discarding the vegetables. Leave to become cold. Skim the fat off the top.
To Freeze: Wrap the joint in foil. Place the stock in a rigid freezer container and cover. Freeze both.
To Serve: Allow to thaw in the refrigerator overnight. Serve the meat thinly sliced with the chopped jellied stock, pickles and salads.

SWEET AND SOUR BACON STEAKS

4 bacon steaks
a little oil
4 teaspoons demerara sugar
Sauce:
1 tablespoon oil
1 onion, peeled and finely chopped
1 tablespoon plain flour
1 x 225 g (8 oz) can pineapple rings
1 tablespoon soy sauce
1 tablespoon wine vinegar
1 tablespoon tomato ketchup
salt
freshly ground black pepper
To serve:
100 g (4 oz) long-grain rice
50 g (2 oz) frozen peas
50 g (2 oz) frozen sweetcorn kernels

Preparation time: 20 minutes
Cooking time: 30 minutes
Oven: 180°C, 350°F, Gas Mark 4

1. Put the bacon steaks on the rack in a grill pan, brush them with oil and cook under a preheated medium grill for 5 minutes.
2. Turn the steaks, brush with oil and sprinkle with the sugar. Grill until the sugar melts and caramelizes. Remove from the heat and cool.
3. To make the sauce, heat the oil in a saucepan, add the onion and fry until softened. Stir in the flour and cook for 1 minute.
4. Drain the juice from the pineapple. Make up the juice to 300 ml (½ pint) with water. Stir into the pan, then add the soy sauce, wine vinegar and tomato ketchup. Cook, stirring constantly, until the sauce has thickened.
5. Cut the pineapple into chunks and add to the sauce. Add the salt and pepper. Cool.
To Freeze: Pack the steaks and sauce into a rigid freezer container, cover and freeze.
To Serve: Allow to thaw at room temperature for 3-4 hours. Put the steaks and sauce into an ovenproof dish, cover and reheat in a preheated oven until hot and bubbling. Meanwhile, cook the rice in boiling salted water for 8 minutes. Add the peas and sweetcorn and cook for a further 5 minutes. Drain well and serve with the bacon steaks.

Sweet and sour bacon steaks

PAPRIKA PORK

2 tablespoons oil
25 g (1 oz) butter
450 g (1 lb) pork fillet, sliced
1 onion, peeled and chopped
1 garlic clove, peeled and crushed
2 tablespoons paprika
25 g (1 oz) plain flour
150 ml (¼ pint) medium cider
150 ml (¼ pint) beef stock
1 tablespoon tomato purée
salt
freshly ground black pepper
175 g (6 oz) small button mushrooms, halved
150 ml (¼ pint) soured cream, to serve

Preparation time: 15 minutes
Cooking time: 25 minutes

PORK FRIKADELLER WITH RED CABBAGE

340 g (1 lb) lean boneless pork
1 medium onion, peeled
2 tablespoons dry parsley and thyme stuffing mix
1 egg, beaten
salt
freshly ground black pepper
50 g (2 oz) butter
2 tablespoons oil
Red cabbage:
40 g (1½ oz) butter
1 kg (2 lb) red cabbage, cored and finely sliced
40 g (1½ oz) demerara sugar
4 tablespoons water
4 tablespoons wine vinegar
salt
freshly ground black pepper
1 cooking apple, peeled, cored and chopped

Preparation time: 20 minutes, plus chilling
Cooking time: 1½ hours
Oven: 180°C, 350°F, Gas Mark 4

1. Finely mince the pork with the onion. Mix with the dry stuffing, egg and salt and pepper until well blended. With floured hands shape into 8 small oval patties. Chill for 1 hour.
2. Heat the butter and oil in a frying pan, add half the patties and fry over a medium heat for about 8 minutes on each side or until well browned. Remove from the pan and fry the remaining patties in the same way. Cool.
3. To make the red cabbage, melt the butter in a heavy saucepan and add the cabbage, sugar, water and vinegar. Add the salt and pepper. Cover tightly and cook over a low heat for about 1 hour, shaking the pan and stirring occasionally.
4. Add the apples and cook for a further 15 minutes. Allow to cool.
To Freeze: Pack the frikadeller and cabbage in separate freezer containers, cover and freeze.
To Serve: Allow to thaw at room temperature for 4-6 hours. Put the cabbage in a casserole, cover and heat in a preheated oven for about 45 minutes. Place the frikadeller on a greased baking sheet and heat in the oven for 30 minutes. Serve with boiled new potatoes tossed in butter and finely chopped parsley.

Variation:
Serve the frikadeller with mock Sauerkraut instead of Red cabbage. Finely shred hard white cabbage and cook in butter with 1 tablespoon caster sugar, water, white wine vinegar, as above, ½ teaspoon caraway seeds and salt and pepper. Cook as for the red cabbage but be careful that it does not brown.

ABOVE: Paprika pork; BELOW: Pork frikadeller with red cabbage

1. Heat the oil and butter in a heavy saucepan, add the pork slices and brown on both sides. Remove from the pan.
2. Add the onion and garlic to the pan with the paprika and fry for about 2 minutes. Stir in the flour and cook for a further 1 minute.
3. Stir in the cider, stock and tomato purée. Bring to the boil, stirring until thickened and smooth.
4. Add the salt and pepper. Replace the pork. Cover and simmer for 15 minutes. Add the mushrooms and cook for a further 5 minutes. Cool.
To Freeze: Pack in a rigid freezer container, cover and freeze.
To Serve: Allow to thaw at room temperature for 4-6 hours. Return to the saucepan and bring slowly to the boil, stirring from time to time. Stir in the soured cream and heat but do not allow to boil. Taste and adjust the seasoning. Serve with small boiled potatoes and green vegetables.

BACON AND MUSHROOM DUMPLING

Pastry:
175 g (6 oz) self-raising flour
75 g (3 oz) shredded suet
salt
freshly ground white pepper
Filling:
175 g (6 oz) open mushrooms, finely chopped
100 g (4 oz) streaky bacon, rind removed, finely chopped
1 small onion, peeled and finely chopped
1 celery stick, finely chopped
1 teaspoon dried thyme
salt
freshly ground black pepper

Preparation time: 25 minutes
Cooking time: 50 minutes
Oven: 200°C, 400°F, Gas Mark 6

1. To make the pastry, sift the flour into a bowl and stir in the suet, salt and pepper. Add enough water to make a soft, pliable dough.
2. Mix together all the filling ingredients.
3. Roll out the dough to a 25 x 30 cm (10 x 12 inch) oblong and spread the filling over to within 2.5 cm (1 inch) of all the edges.
4. Dampen the edges and roll up, starting from a shorter side. Seal the edges well. Put on a baking sheet.
To Freeze: Open freeze. When solid, wrap in foil and return to the freezer.
To Serve: Unwrap and allow to thaw on a baking sheet at room temperature for 3 hours. Bake in a preheated oven for 40 minutes or until golden brown and crisp. Serve with green vegetables.

LAMB WITH PINEAPPLE

1 kg (2-2½ lb) top of the leg joint of lamb
2 tablespoons oil
12 pickling onions, peeled
40 g (1½ oz) plain flour
¼ teaspoon Chinese 5-spice powder
1 x 225 g (8 oz) can pineapple rings in natural juice
2 tablespoons tomato purée
salt
freshly ground black pepper
225 g (8 oz) tiny button mushrooms
chopped parsley, to garnish

Preparation time: 30 minutes
Cooking time: 1¼ hours
Oven: 180°C, 350°F, Gas Mark 4

This recipe requires lean meat so use the leg meat rather than a cheaper cut. A small joint cut from the top of the leg of lamb will give enough meat for this dish, plus a bone to boil for the stock. Chinese 5-spice powder is now available in most shops. If you cannot obtain it use a pinch of ground nutmeg and coriander, 1-2 teaspoons of soy sauce and a tablespoon of dry sherry.

1. Cut the meat off the bone. Remove skin and fat and boil these with the bone for stock. Cut the meat into cubes.
2. Heat the oil in a frying pan, add the onions and fry until lightly coloured. Add the lamb cubes and cook until sealed and lightly browned. Lift out with a slotted spoon and put into a 1.75 litre (3 pint) casserole.
3. Stir the flour and spice into the pan juices and cook for 1 minute. Drain the juice from the pineapple. Make up the juice with lamb stock to 450 ml (¾ pint) and add to the pan. Stir until thickened and smooth. Add the tomato purée and salt and pepper, then pour into the casserole.
4. Cover and cook in a preheated oven for 1¼ hours or until the lamb is tender. Stir in the mushrooms and pineapple cut into chunks. Cool.
To Freeze: Pour into a rigid freezer container, cover and freeze.
To Serve: Allow to thaw at room temperature for 6-7 hours. Return to the casserole, cover and reheat in a preheated oven for about 45 minutes or until hot and bubbling. Taste and adjust the seasoning and sprinkle with parsley. Serve with rice and green vegetables.

Variation:
Omit the pineapple and substitute a 1 x 450 g (16 oz) can of green flageolet beans plus 1 tablespoon of chopped fresh mint. Serve with crispy noodles crumbled on top.

LEEK PIE

Serves 6
Pastry:
350 g (12 oz) plain flour
salt
75 g (3 oz) lard
75 g (3 oz) butter or hard margarine
Filling:
100 g (4 oz) bacon, rind removed, chopped
450 g (1 lb) leeks, sliced into rings
3 eggs, beaten
salt
freshly ground black pepper

Preparation time: 30 minutes
Cooking time: 1¼ hours
Oven: 200°C, 400°F, Gas Mark 6;
180°C, 350°F, Gas Mark 4

1. To make the pastry, sift the flour and salt into a bowl and rub in the fats until the mixture resembles crumbs. Add enough cold water to mix to a firm dough. Roll out three-quarters of the dough and use to line a 900 ml (1½ pint) freezerproof pie dish.
2. Cook the bacon in a frying pan over a gentle heat until the fat begins to run. Add the leeks and cook for a further 5 minutes, stirring continuously, until the leeks have softened. Allow to cool slightly. Transfer to the pastry case.
3. Mix the eggs with salt and pepper and pour into the pie, reserving a little egg for glazing the pastry. Tilt the pie to ensure the egg runs round evenly inside.
4. Roll out the rest of the dough to make a lid. Place on the dish and seal the edges. Trim and flute. Use the dough trimmings to make decorative leaves and a central rose. Brush with a little water to secure in place.
5. Bake in a preheated oven for 20 minutes. Brush all over the pastry lid with the reserved egg. Reduce the oven temperature and bake the pie for a further 35-40 minutes. Cover the pastry with a piece of foil if it gets too browned. Cool.
To Freeze: Open freeze, then wrap in foil and return to the freezer.
To Serve: Allow to thaw in the refrigerator overnight. Serve cold, or warm in a preheated oven (180°C, 350°F, Gas Mark 4) for about 20 minutes.

Leek pie; Lamb with pineapple

LAMB CURRY

4 tablespoons oil
1 large onion, peeled and chopped
1 garlic clove, peeled and crushed
1 cm (½ inch) piece fresh root ginger, peeled and finely
    chopped
50 g (2 oz) creamed coconut
2-4 teaspoons curry powder
600 ml (1 pint) beef stock
salt
freshly ground black pepper
450 g (1 lb) boneless lamb, cubed
¼ teaspoon ground coriander
2 tablespoons apricot jam

Preparation time: 20 minutes
Cooking time: 1½ hours

Everyone who likes curry has their own favourite recipe.
This basic sauce can be used for meat, prawns or egg. You
can vary the sweetness or 'hotness' to your taste.

1. Heat 2 tablespoons of the oil in a saucepan, add the
onion and garlic and fry until lightly browned. Stir in the
ginger and coconut and cook gently for 2 minutes.
2. Stir in the curry powder, stock and salt and pepper.
Bring to the boil and simmer for 15 minutes.
3. Meanwhile, heat the remaining oil in a frying pan.
Add the lamb, season with salt, pepper and coriander
and fry until well browned on all sides.
4. Put the lamb into the sauce and cook over a very low
heat for about 1 hour or until tender. Stir in the jam. Cool.
To Freeze: Pack in a rigid polythene container, cover and
freeze.
To Serve: Allow to thaw at room temperature for 4-6
hours. Return to the pan and slowly bring to the boil,
stirring occasionally. Taste and adjust the seasoning.
Serve with rice, sliced tomato and onion salad, and
cucumber grated into plain unsweetened yogurt.

If you have a coffee grinder or small mill you can
make your own curry powder, varying the degree of
sweetness or hotness to your own taste; try 4 teaspoons ground coriander; 1 teaspoon ground
turmeric; 2 teaspoons ground cumin, 1 teaspoon
pepper, 2-4 teaspoons chilli powder and 1 teaspoon
ground cloves.

   Fresh root ginger is much lighter in flavour than
preserved or ground ginger. To keep it fresh, peel
and slice the root and store in a tightly covered jar
with a little dry sherry for 1-2 months.

LAMB ANNA

100 g (4 oz) pork sausagemeat
1 egg, beaten
4 slices of bread, made into breadcrumbs
1 teaspoon dried mixed herbs
1 teaspoon French mustard
salt
freshly ground black pepper
2 breasts of lamb, boned and trimmed of excess fat
1 large potato, peeled and diced
2 carrots, peeled and sliced
1 parsnip, peeled and diced
1 turnip, peeled and diced
1 onion, peeled and chopped
2 tablespoons plain flour
300 ml (½ pint) beef stock

Preparation time: 30 minutes
Cooking time: 2 hours
Oven: 160°C, 325°F, Gas Mark 3

This is an excellent way of using a cheaper cut of meat. It
is good served cold too: use the vegetables to make a soup
and have the cold meat with salad.

1. Mix together the sausagemeat, egg, breadcrumbs,
herbs, mustard, and salt and pepper. Spread evenly over
the meat. Roll up tightly and tie with string.
2. Put all the vegetables into a large roasting tin and
sprinkle with the flour, salt and pepper. Pour in the
stock. Lay the rolled meat on top.
3. Cover with foil and cook in a preheated oven for 2
hours. Cool.
To Freeze: Wrap the meat rolls in foil. Pack the vegetables in a rigid freezer container and cover. Freeze both.
To Serve: Allow to thaw at room temperature for 3-4
hours. Slice the meat thickly. To serve hot, put the
vegetables into an oblong ovenproof serving dish and
arrange the meat slices on top. Cover with foil and heat in
a preheated oven (180°C, 350°F, Gas Mark 4) for about 30
minutes or until heated through. Serve with baked jacket
potatoes, green vegetables and mint sauce.

Lamb Anna

CANTERBURY HOT-POT

2 carrots, peeled and chopped
1 small swede, peeled and chopped
1 small parsnip, peeled and chopped
1 small turnip, peeled and chopped
salt
2 tablespoons oil
8 lamb chops, trimmed of fat
1 onion, peeled and chopped
freshly ground black pepper
3 tablespoons mint sauce
750 g (1½ lb) potatoes, peeled, parboiled and sliced

Preparation time: 35 minutes
Cooking time: 1½-1¾ hours
Oven: 180°C, 350°F, Gas Mark 4

1. Put the carrots, swede, parsnip and turnip into a saucepan, just cover with salted water and bring to the boil. Simmer for 3 minutes. Drain, reserving 300 ml (½ pint) of the liquid.
2. Put the vegetables into the bottom of a 1.75 litre (3 pint) freezerproof casserole.
3. Heat the oil in a frying pan, add the chops and fry on each side to seal and brown lightly. Remove. Add the onion to the pan and fry until softened.
4. Scatter the onion over the vegetables in the casserole and lay the chops on top. Add salt and pepper. Mix the mint sauce with the reserved vegetable cooking liquid and pour over.
5. Cover with the potatoes, overlapping each other. Brush with any fat left in the frying pan. Cool.
To Freeze: Cover, wrap and freeze.
To Serve: Allow to thaw at room temperature for 3-4 hours. Uncover and cook in a preheated oven for 1-1½ hours or until the meat and potatoes are tender and the potatoes are browned. Serve with a green vegetable.

CHICKEN LIVER PAN-FRY

2 tablespoons oil
2 streaky bacon rashers, rind removed, chopped
1 onion, peeled and finely chopped
1 small green pepper, cored, seeded and sliced
450 g (1 lb) chicken livers, trimmed
100 g (4 oz) mushrooms, quartered
1-2 teaspoons dried sage
To serve:
6 tablespoons dry vermouth or white wine
salt
freshly ground black pepper

Preparation time: 10 minutes
Cooking time: 15 minutes

1. Heat the oil in a frying pan, add the bacon and onion and fry until lightly browned.
2. Add the green pepper and chicken livers and cook for about 5 minutes. Stir in the mushrooms and sage and cook for a further 5 minutes. Cool.
To Freeze: Pack in a rigid freezer container, cover and freeze.
To Serve: Allow to thaw at room temperature for 6-7 hours. Return to the pan, add the vermouth or wine and slowly bring to the boil, stirring occasionally. Season to taste with salt and pepper, then serve with plain boiled white or brown rice and a mixed salad.

LIVER STROGANOFF

50 g (2 oz) butter
1 tablespoon oil
1 large onion, peeled and thinly sliced
450 g (1 lb) lambs' liver, cut into thin strips
1 tablespoon tomato purée
150 ml (¼ pint) beef stock
1 teaspoon French mustard
150 ml (¼ pint) soured cream, to serve
salt
freshly ground black pepper

Preparation time: 10 minutes
Cooking time: 15 minutes

1. Heat the butter and oil in a frying pan, add the onion and fry gently until softened but not coloured.
2. Add the liver and cook gently for about 8 minutes.
3. Mix the tomato purée with the stock, add to the pan and cook for 2 minutes. Stir in the mustard. Cool.
To Freeze: Pack in a rigid freezer container, cover and freeze.
To Serve: Allow to thaw at room temperature for 3-4 hours. Return to the pan and slowly bring to the boil, stirring occasionally. Stir in the soured cream and season to taste with salt and pepper. Heat through gently, without boiling. Serve immediately with vegetables and/or plain boiled rice.

OXTAIL BRAISE

1 oxtail, cut into joints
40 g (1½ oz) plain flour
salt
freshly ground black pepper
2 tablespoons oil
900 ml (1½ pints) beef stock
1 tablespoon creamed horseradish
1 large onion, peeled and sliced
2 carrots, peeled and sliced
2 celery sticks, sliced
1 small parsnip, peeled and diced
1 bay leaf

Dumplings:
75 g (3 oz) fresh wholemeal breadcrumbs
1 teaspoon dried mixed herbs
1 tablespoon shredded suet
2 tablespoons plain wholemeal flour
1 egg, beaten
salt
freshly ground black pepper

Preparation time: 40 minutes
Cooking time: 3 hours
Oven: 160°C, 325°F, Gas Mark 3

FROM THE LEFT: Chicken liver pan-fry; Liver stroganoff

Oxtail is a cheap cut which is ideally suited to braising. The meat becomes tender and the flavour is superb.

1. Coat the oxtail pieces in flour seasoned with salt and pepper. Heat the oil in a frying pan, add the oxtail pieces and fry until well browned all over. Lift out with a slotted spoon and set aside.
2. Add any remaining seasoned flour to the frying pan and cook, stirring continuously, for 1 minute or until browned. Stir in the stock and cook until thickened and smooth. Stir in the horseradish.
3. Put all the vegetables into the bottom of a 2.25 litre (4 pint) casserole. Add the bay leaf and lay the pieces of oxtail on top.
4. Pour the horseradish sauce over the oxtail. Cover and cook in a preheated oven for 3 hours. Cool, then skim off any fat from the surface.
5. To make the dumplings, mix together all the ingredients, then form into small balls.
To Freeze: Put the stew into a rigid freezer container, cover and freeze. Open freeze the dumplings on a baking sheet. When solid, pack in a polythene bag or container and return to the freezer.
To Serve: Allow to thaw in the refrigerator overnight. Put the stew back into the casserole, cover and reheat in a preheated oven (180°C, 350°F, Gas Mark 4) for about 1 hour. Add the dumplings and cook for a further 20 minutes or until they are risen and cooked through. Discard the bay leaf and serve.

HADDOCK AND ANCHOVY PIE

350 g (12 oz) haddock fillet
150 ml (¼ pint) milk
150 ml (¼ pint) water
25 g (1 oz) butter
25 g (1 oz) plain flour
4 anchovy fillets, chopped
1 hard-boiled egg, finely chopped
salt
freshly ground black pepper
1 x 215 g (7½ oz) packet frozen puff pastry, thawed
beaten egg, to glaze

Preparation time: 30 minutes
Cooking time: 45 minutes
Oven: 200°C, 400°F, Gas Mark 6

If you find the salty flavour of anchovy too strong, use chopped parsley and some lemon rind instead. Make sure the egg is very finely chopped as freezing tends to toughen the white.

1. Put the haddock in a saucepan with the milk and water. Cover and poach for 10 minutes.
2. Lift the fish from the pan. Remove skin and bones and flake the flesh. Reserve the poaching liquid in the pan.
3. Mix together the butter and flour to make a paste. Stir into the poaching liquid, in small pieces, and slowly bring to the boil, stirring until thickened and smooth. Add the fish, anchovies, egg, and salt and pepper. Cool.
5. Roll out the pastry dough to a 30 cm (12 inch) square. Trim the edges. Turn so a corner is pointing towards you.
6. Put the fish mixture in the centre of the square. Fold the pastry like an envelope – the bottom corner to the centre, the 2 side corners to the centre, then the top corner down to cover. Brush all edges with beaten egg as you fold, and press to seal.
To Freeze: Put the pie on a baking sheet and open freeze. When solid, wrap in foil and return to the freezer.
To Serve: Unwrap and allow to thaw on a baking sheet at room temperature for 2-3 hours. Brush with beaten egg and bake in a preheated oven for 45-50 minutes or until well risen, golden brown and heated through.

Haddock and anchovy pie; Baked stuffed herrings

BAKED STUFFED HERRINGS

4 fresh herrings
Stuffing:
25 g (1 oz) butter
1 small onion, peeled and chopped
1 small cooking apple, peeled, cored and grated
grated rind and juice of ½ lemon
1 tablespoon chopped parsley
40 g (1½ oz) fine oatmeal
salt
freshly ground black pepper
6 tablespoons apple juice
To garnish
lemon slices
parsley sprigs

Preparation time: 10 minutes, plus boning
Cooking time: 45 minutes
Oven: 160°C, 325°F, Gas Mark 3

To save time you can buy the herrings already boned, but it is not difficult to bone fresh ones yourself.

1. Scrape the scales off the fish with a knife, working from tail to head. Cut off the head behind the gills, until the knife just cuts through the backbone. Pull the head and guts away from the body. Using scissors, cut off the fins and tail.
2. Cut along the underside of the fish, to the vent. Lift out any roe and reserve, then pull away the silver thread attached to the spine. Turn the fish skin side up, spread it flat, then press firmly on the backbone until it is flattened. Turn the fish over and lift out the loosened bone, taking out all the small bones with it.
3. Rinse and dry the fish, rubbing with a little salt to remove any black patches on the flesh.
4. To make the stuffing, melt the butter in a frying pan, add the onion and fry until softened. Add the rest of the stuffing ingredients, together with any fish roe, chopped, and season with salt and pepper. Mix well.
5. Lay the herrings flat on a board, skin side down. Divide the stuffing between them and roll up starting at the tail end.
6. Put the fish rolls into an ovenproof freezer dish that will hold them snugly. Spoon over 4 tablespoons of the apple juice.
7. Cover with buttered greaseproof paper and foil and bake in a preheated oven for about 45 minutes. Cool.
To Freeze: Cover with fresh greaseproof paper and foil and freeze.
To Serve: Allow to thaw at room temperature for 3-4 hours. Add the remaining apple juice, cover and place in a preheated oven (180°C, 350°F, Gas Mark 4) for about 25 minutes or until hot through. Garnish with lemon slices and parsley.

Scrape the scales off with a knife.

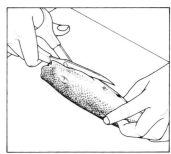
Cut the belly to the small vent.

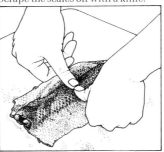
Loosening the backbone.

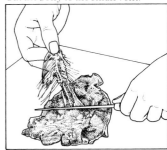
Carefully removing the backbone.

SMOKEY FISH CAKES

350 g (12 oz) smoked haddock fillet
150 ml (¼ pint) milk
225 g (8 oz) potatoes, peeled and freshly cooked
25 g (1 oz) butter
1 tablespoon chopped parsley
freshly ground black pepper
1 small packet smokey bacon-favoured potato crisps
4 tablespoons dry breadcrumbs
1 egg, beaten
oil for deep drying

Preparation time: 40 minutes, plus chilling
Cooking time: 15 minutes

1. Place the fish in a saucepan with the milk. Poach for about 10 minutes. Drain, reserving 2 tablespoons of the liquid. Remove any skin and bones from the fish and flake the flesh finely.
2. Mash the potatoes with the reserved liquid and butter, then mix in the fish and parsley. Add the pepper. With lightly floured hands, form into 8 round cakes. Chill until firm.
3. Put the crisps into a paper bag and crush finely with a rolling pin. Mix with the breadcrumbs.
4. Dip the fish cakes into the beaten egg to coat, then cover evenly with the crumb mixture, pressing it on all over.
To Freeze: Open freeze on a baking sheet. When solid, pack in a rigid container, cover and return to the freezer.
To Serve: Deep fry from frozen in hot oil (190°C, 375°F) for about 8 minutes or until golden and heated through. Serve with green vegetables or salads.

COLD POACHED TROUT WITH HAZELNUT MAYONNAISE

4 x 200 g (7 oz) trout, cleaned
2 bay leaves
few parsley stalks
salt
freshly ground black pepper
Hazelnut mayonnaise:
1 egg
100 g (4 oz) ground hazelnuts
4 tablespoons wine vinegar
4-6 tablespoons water
salt
freshly ground black pepper
To serve:
1 tablespoon aspic jelly powder
parsley sprigs
cucumber balls or small cubes

Preparation time: 20 minutes
Cooking time: 10 minutes
Oven: 180°C, 350°F, Gas Mark 4

Some people do not like to see the heads on cooked fish. They can be removed after thawing, before glazing.

1. Trim the trout fins. Put into a large shallow dish or roasting tin big enough to hold them in one layer.
2. Cover with boiling water and add the bay leaves, parsley stalks, salt and pepper. Cover with foil and cook in a preheated oven for 10 minutes. Leave to cool in the water, then drain. Slit the skin from head to tail along the back and belly and carefully remove the skin.
3. To make the mayonnaise, put the egg into a blender and add the hazelnuts, vinegar and 4 tablespoons of water. Blend together to make a mayonnaise consistency, adding more water if it is too stiff. Add the salt and pepper.
To Freeze: Pack the fish and mayonnaise in separate rigid freezer containers, cover and freeze.
To Serve: Allow to thaw in the refrigerator overnight. Make up the aspic jelly as instructed on the packet. Put the fish on a serving dish and brush with the aspic to glaze. Garnish with parsley sprigs and small cubes or balls of peeled cucumber. Serve with the hazelnut mayonnaise.

SEAFOOD CONTINENTAL WITH SPICED RICE

2 tablespoons oil
2 garlic cloves, peeled and crushed
450 g (1 lb) tomatoes, skinned and chopped
2 canned pimentos, drained and chopped
¼ teaspoon dried oregano
3 tablespoons white wine
225 g (8 oz) cod fillet, skinned and cubed
175 g (6 oz) uncooked peeled scampi
100 g (4 oz) peeled prawns
chopped parsley, to garnish (optional)
Spiced Rice:
1 tablespoon oil
6 cardamom pods
7 cm (3 inch) cinnamon stick
175 g (6 oz) long-grain rice
4 tablespoons boiling water
salt

Preparation time: 30 minutes
Cooking time: 30 minutes

1. Heat the oil in a saucepan, add the garlic and fry gently for 1 minute. Stir in the tomatoes, pimentos, oregano and wine. Cover and cook gently for 20 minutes.
2. Add the fish and shellfish, cover again and cook for a further 10 minutes. Cool.
3. Heat the oil in another saucepan, add the spices and stir for a moment. Add the rice, water and salt and bring to the boil Simmer for about 10 minutes or until the water has been absorbed and the rice is tender. Cool.
To Freeze: Pack the fish mixture and rice separately in rigid freezer containers, cover and freeze.
To Serve: Allow to thaw at room temperature for 3-4 hours. As the fish has been fully cooked before freezing be careful not to overcook it at this stage. Return the fish mixture to the pan and slowly bring to the boil, stirring occasionally. Place the rice in another saucepan with 2 tablespoons water. Cover and heat gently until the water has been absorbed. Remove the spices. Serve the fish on the rice, sprinkled with chopped parsley, (if using).

COD STEAKS WITH NUTTY CHEESE TOPPING

4 cod steaks
50 g (2 oz) soft margarine or softened butter
100 g (4 oz) Cheddar cheeese, grated
50 g (2 oz) salted peanuts, chopped
2 teaspoons milk
watercress, to garnish

Preparation time: 10 minutes
Cooking time: 15-20 minutes
Oven: 180°C, 350°F, Gas Mark 4

Try to buy cod steaks that are cut from near the tail end of the fish with flesh all round the bone.

1. Put the cod steaks in a buttered grill pan and seal under a preheated medium grill for 5 minutes. Turn the steaks over.
2. Blend together all the rest of the ingredients and spread on top of each steak.
3. Grill gently for a further 12-15 minutes or until the cheese topping has lightly browned. Cool.
To Freeze: Pack in a rigid freezer container, cover and freeze.
To Serve: Allow to thaw at room temperature for 3-4 hours. Put in an ovenproof dish, cover with foil and reheat in a preheated oven for about 20 minutes or until heated through. Finish under the grill to brown the top. Garnish with watercress, and serve with baked tomatoes and mashed potatoes.

Cold poached trout with hazelnut mayonnaise;
Seafood continental with spiced rice

SPECIAL OCCASIONS

NOISETTES OF LAMB WITH ROSEMARY AND BAKED DUMPLINGS

Serves 6
1 tablespoon dried rosemary
50 g (2 oz) butter, softened
2 chicken stock cubes
2 loins of lamb, containing 6 chops each, boned
Dumplings:
100 g (4 oz) self-raising flour, sifted
50 g (2 oz) shredded suet
1 egg, beaten
about 100 ml (3½ fl oz) milk
salt
freshly ground black pepper
To serve:
1 garlic clove, peeled
a little oil

Preparation time: 20 minutes
Cooking time: 25 minutes
Oven: 200°C, 400°F, Gas Mark 6

Ask the butcher to bone the meat (make sure he gives you the bones) and to leave the meat flat. These noisettes are ideal for a dinner party. They cook quickly, taste delicious and are not too heavy in a three course meal.

1. Pound the rosemary to a powder in a mortar with a pestle or in a bowl with the end of a rolling pin. Beat in the butter and crumbled stock cubes.
2. Spread the rosemary mixture over the inside of the meat. Roll up and tie the joint in 4 places with string.
3. To make the dumplings, mix together all the ingredients to make a soft dough. Shape into 12 even sized balls.
To Freeze: Wrap the meat in foil and freeze. Open freeze the dumplings on a baking sheet. When solid, pack in a polythene bag and return to the freezer.
To Serve: Allow the meat to thaw in the refrigerator for 6-8 hours. Unwrap the meat and place in an oiled roasting tin with the frozen dumplings. Rub the meat with the garlic and brush the meat and dumplings with oil. Cook in a preheated oven (200°C, 400°F, Gas Mark 6) for about 25 minutes. The meat juices should run slightly pink when pierced with a pointed knife. The dumplings should be risen, golden and crisp. Cut the meat into 12 noisettes, and serve with the dumplings, vegetables and redcurrant jelly.

LAMB GUARD OF HONOUR

Serves 6
Stuffing:
50 g (2 oz) dried apricots
25 g (1 oz) butter
2 medium leeks, about 350 g (12 oz), cut into rings
75 g (3 oz) long-grain rice
450 ml (¾ pint) chicken stock
2 tablespoons pine nuts
40 g (1½ oz) sultanas
salt
freshly ground black pepper
2 best ends of lamb, prepared as a Guard of Honour
a little oil

Preparation time: 20 minutes, plus soaking
Cooking time: 20 minutes
Oven: 200°C, 400°F, Gas Mark 6

A good butcher will prepare a Guard of Honour for you if you give him a few days' notice. This stuffing could also be used for a Crown of Lamb. Cutlet frills on the bone ends look very professional but if you can't buy them make little foil ones instead.

1. To make the stuffing, soak the apricots in water for 30 minutes, then drain and chop. Melt the butter in a saucepan, add the leeks and fry until just softened. Stir in the rice and fry for 1 minute.
2. Stir in the stock. Bring to the boil, then cover and cook until the rice is tender and all the liquid has been absorbed, about 12-15 minutes.
3. Stir in the pine nuts, apricots and sultanas. Add salt and pepper and cool.
4. Stand the lamb on a sheet of heavy-duty freezer foil. Put the stuffing into the middle, under the crossed bones.
To Freeze: Overwrap the bone ends with freezer film or greaseproof paper. Wrap the whole well in the foil and freeze.
To Serve: Allow to thaw, wrapped in the refrigerator for 6-8 hours. Put into a roasting tin and unwrap the top of the foil, leaving the ends of the joint covered to protect the rice. Brush the meat with oil, season with salt and pepper and cook in a preheated oven for about 40 minutes or until crisp and browned. Put cutlet frills on the ends of the bones and serve, with redcurrant jelly.

Lamb guard of honour

ITALIAN LAMB

8 lean best end lamb chops, chined
25 g (1 oz) butter
½ teaspoon dried oregano
2 large onions, peeled and thickly sliced
1 small red pepper, cored, seeded and cut into rings
1 small green pepper, cored, seeded and cut into rings
100 g (4 oz) courgettes, sliced
4 large tomatoes, skinned and sliced
1 teaspoon sugar
salt
freshly ground black pepper
300 ml (½ pint) red wine

Preparation time: 30 minutes
Cooking time: 1 hour
Oven: 180°C, 350°F, Gas Mark 4

1. Remove the bones from the chops and shape them into neat rounds, securing with a wooden cocktail stick or string.
2. Rub a deep freezerproof casserole thickly with the butter and sprinkle with oregano. Put the onions into the bottom and arrange the peppers, courgettes and tomatoes on top in layers. Sprinkle with the sugar, salt and pepper and pour over the wine.
3. Arrange the chops on top. Cover and cook in a preheated oven for about 1 hour. Cool. Skim off excess fat.
To Freeze: Cover and freeze.
To Serve: Allow to thaw at room temperature for 4-6 hours. Reheat in a preheated oven for about 45 minutes or until hot. Serve with new potatoes and a fennel salad.

The following three stuffings are unusual variations suitable for chicken or turkey.

BACON AND BRAZIL NUT STUFFING

Sufficient for 1 x 1.5-1.75 kg (3-4½ lb) chicken.
Double the quantities for 1 x 4.5-5.5 kg (10-12 lb) turkey.
1 bacon hock, soaked in cold water for 24 hours and drained
1 small onion, peeled
100 g (4 oz) fresh brown breadcrumbs
2 tomatoes, skinned and chopped
1 dessert apple, peeled, cored and grated
50 g (2 oz) brazil nuts, chopped
2 tablespoons chopped fresh herbs
1 egg, beaten
1 tablespoon shredded suet
freshly ground black pepper

Preparation time: 15 minutes

1. Remove the skin from the bacon. Take the meat from the bone and reserve 175 g (6 oz) of it. (Use the rest for another dish.) Mince the reserved meat with the onion. Stir in the rest of the ingredients.
To Freeze: Put into a rigid freezer container, cover and freeze.
To Use: Allow to thaw at room temperature for 3-4 hours. Use to stuff a chicken or turkey before roasting.

PRUNE AND ALMOND STUFFING

Sufficient for 1 x 1.5-1.75 kg (3-4½ lb) chicken.
Double the quantities for 1 x 4.5-5.5 kg (10-12 lb) turkey.
25 g (1 oz) butter
1 small onion, peeled and chopped
100 g (4 oz) minced pork
100 g (4 oz) seedless raisins, chopped
50 g (2 oz) rolled oats
50 g (2 oz) blanched almonds, chopped
1 egg, beaten
salt
freshly ground black pepper

Preparation time: 10 minutes

CRANBERRY RICE STUFFING

Sufficient for 1 x 1.5-1.75 kg (3-4½ lb) chicken.
Double the quantities for 1 x 4.5-5.5 kg (10-12 lb) turkey
25 g (1 oz) butter
4 spring onions, finely sliced
1 chicken or turkey liver, chopped
2 celery sticks, finely sliced
50 g (2 oz) long-grain rice, cooked and drained
3 tablespoons cranberry sauce
1 egg, beaten
salt
freshly ground black pepper

Preparation time: 15 minutes

1. Melt the butter in a frying pan, add the spring onions, liver and celery and fry for 5 minutes. Add the rest of the ingredients and mix well. Cool.
To Freeze: Put into a rigid freezer container, cover and freeze.
To Use: Allow to thaw at room temperature for 3-4 hours. Use to stuff a chicken or turkey before roasting.

1. Melt the butter in a frying pan, add the onion and fry until softened. Add the remaining ingredients and mix well. Cool.
To Freeze: Put into a rigid freezer container, cover and freeze.
To Use: Allow to thaw at room temperature for 3-4 hours. Use to stuff a chicken or turkey before roasting.

Italian lamb

ROAST STUFFED CHICKEN

Serves 6
1 x 1.5 kg (3 lb) oven-ready chicken
350 kg (12 oz) lean minced pork
1 small onion, peeled and minced
40 g (1½ oz) fresh breadcrumbs
2 eggs, beaten
½ teaspoon dried tarragon
salt
freshly ground black pepper
50 g (2 oz) butter
225 g (8 oz) chicken livers, trimmed
watercress, to garnish

Preparation time: 45 minutes
Cooking time: 5-10 minutes
Oven: 190°C, 375°F, Gas Mark 5

It is not difficult to remove the body carcass from a chicken – the tricky part is taking out the leg and wing bones; in this recipe they are left in to keep the bird in its usual shape. It is impressive to carve in front of guests; cut off the legs and wings, then slice across the body.

1. With a small sharp knife, cut along the length of the backbone, through the parson's nose. Cutting close to the bone, gradually ease away the meat and skin from round the body carcass. When you reach the joint of the thigh bone and the body, break it away from the socket, leaving the bones in the leg. Do the same with the wing joints.

2. When the breast bone has been cut free (take care not to slit the skin over the top of the breast bone) lift out the body carcass. Lay the chicken flat, skin side down and arrange the chicken meat evenly.

3. Mix together the pork, onion, breadcrumbs, eggs, herbs, and salt and pepper.

4. Melt 25 g (1 oz) of the butter in a frying pan, add the chicken livers and fry gently for 5 minutes. Chop the livers finely.

5. Spread half the pork mixture down the centre of the chicken. Spread the chicken livers on top and cover with the rest of the pork mixture.

7. Bring the cut edges of the chicken together again and sew up with needle and cotton to enclose the stuffing completely. Mould the bird to its usual shape and tie with string to hold the legs and wings in place.

To Freeze: Wrap in foil and freeze.

To Serve: Allow to thaw in the refrigerator for 12 hours. Put in a roasting tin, spread with the remaining butter, season with salt and pepper and cover with foil. Roast in a preheated oven for 1½ hours, then remove the foil and roast for a further 20 minutes. Serve hot with vegetables. If you prefer to serve the chicken cold it can be cooked before freezing. Cool, wrap and freeze. Thaw for 12 hours in the refrigerator garnish with watercress and serve sliced with salads.

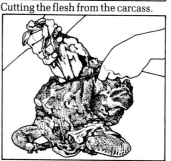
Cutting the flesh from the carcass.

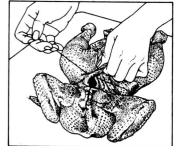
Breaking the thigh joint.

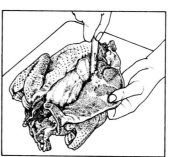
Cutting free the carcass.

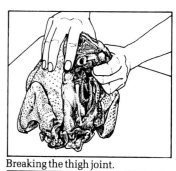
Sewing up the chicken.

Roast stuffed chicken; Anniversary turkey.

ANNIVERSARY TURKEY

Pastry:
175 g (6 oz) plain flour
pinch of salt
100 g (4 oz) butter or hard margarine
100 g (4 oz) full fat soft cheese
beaten egg, to glaze
Filling:
2 skinless, boneless, turkey breasts, about 225 g (8 oz) each
25 g (1 oz) butter, melted
3 tablespoons ground almonds
3 tablespoons cranberry sauce
2 teaspoons grated onion
salt
freshly ground black pepper

Preparation time: 45 minutes, plus chilling
Cooking time: 20 minutes
Oven: 220°C, 425°F, Gas Mark 7

These are rather fun to make for a wedding anniversary dinner party or for Valentines Day.

1. To make the pastry, sift the flour and salt into a bowl and rub in the butter or margarine until the mixture resembles crumbs. Mix in the cheese. Knead to a soft dough, then wrap in foil and chill for 1 hour.
2. Lay the turkey breasts flat on a board. With a sharp knife, split them open lengthways, starting from the rounded side, not cutting all the way through. Open out and flatten a little to make a heart shape.
3. Place the turkey 'hearts' on a grill rack, brush with melted butter and grill gently for about 10 minutes on each side. Cool.
4. Mix together the almonds, cranberry sauce and onion. Add salt and pepper.
5. Halve the dough. Roll out 1 piece to a rectangle about 2½ times the width of 1 turkey 'heart' and 1½ times its length. Cut the rectangle in half. Lay the turkey breast on 1 piece and cut out a heart shape round it, about 2.5 cm (1 inch) bigger all round than the breast. Cut a similar heart shape from the other piece of dough for the top. Spread half the cranberry mixture on the turkey, cover with the dough top, and seal and crimp the edges. Put on a baking sheet. Repeat with the rest of the dough and the other turkey 'heart'.
6. Make decorative leaves or the initials of the anniversary guests with the pastry trimmings. Moisten with a little water to keep in place.
To Freeze: Open freeze on the baking sheet. When solid, wrap in foil and return to the freezer.
To Serve: Allow to thaw, unwrapped, on a baking sheet at room temperature for 3-4 hours. Brush with beaten egg and bake in a preheated oven for 35-40 minutes or until golden, risen and cooked. Serve with hot cranberry sauce, flamed with a little brandy.

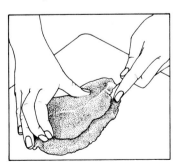

Cutting the breast almost in two.

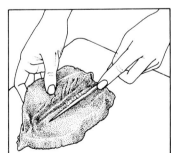

Opening out the breast to form a heart shape.

PIGEON AND STEAK PIE

Serves 6
4 oven-ready pigeons
1 onion, peeled and chopped
1 bouquet garni
salt
freshly ground black pepper
2 tablespoons oil
12 small pickling onions, peeled
225 g (8 oz) lean braising steak, sliced
40 g (1½ oz) lean braising steak, sliced
40 g (1½ oz) plain flour
½ teaspoon dried mixed herbs
150 ml (¼ pint) dry red wine
1 tablespoon plum or apricot jam
Pastry:
175 g (6 oz) self-raising flour
75 g (3 oz) shredded suet
salt
white pepper
about 6 tablespoons water
beaten egg, to glaze

Preparation time: 30 minutes
Cooking time: 3 hours
Oven: 200°C, 400°F, Gas Mark 6

Make the stock for this pie the day before.

1. With a sharp knife, remove the breasts from the pigeons. Skin the breasts and slice each into 3 lengthways.
2. Put the carcasses into a large saucepan, cover with water and add the chopped onion, bouquet garni, and salt and pepper. Bring to the boil, cover and simmer for 1½ hours. Strain the stock and reserve 300 ml (½ pint).
3. Heat the oil in a frying pan, add the pickling onions and fry until lightly browned. Lift out and put in a heavy saucepan. Add the pigeon meat and steak to the frying pan and fry until well sealed. Add to the saucepan.
4. Stir the flour and herbs into the juices in the frying pan. Cook for 1 minute, then stir in the wine, reserved stock and jam. Cook, stirring, until thickened. Add salt and pepper. Transfer to the saucepan, cover and cook gently, stirring occasionally, for about 1¼ hours or until the meat is very tender. Cool.
5. Sift the flour into a bowl and stir in the suet and salt and pepper. Add enough water to make a soft dough. Put the meat mixture into a 1.2 litre (2 pint) freezerproof pie dish with a pie funnel in the centre. Roll out the dough to make a lid. Place on the dish, trim and flute the edges. Decorate with pastry leaves. Brush with beaten egg.
To Freeze: Open freeze, wrap in foil.
To Serve: Unwrap the pie, place on a baking sheet and bake from frozen in a preheated oven for 1¼ hours or until the pastry is well browned and the filling is hot and bubbling.

PHEASANT WITH APPLES AND CREAM

1 oven-ready hen pheasant
25 g (1 oz) butter
1 tablespoon oil
1 medium onion, peeled and finely chopped
100 g (4 oz) green streaky bacon, rind removed, chopped
2 dessert apples, peeled, cored and sliced
150 ml (¼ pint) apple juice
salt
freshly ground black pepper
To Serve:
2 dessert apples, cored and cut into rings
2 tablespoons soft brown sugar
50 g (2 oz) butter
2 tablespoons Calvados, warmed
150 ml (¼ pint) double cream

Preparation time: 20 minutes
Cooking time: 1¼ hours
Oven: 190°C, 375°F, Gas Mark 5

1. Wipe the pheasant and trim the legs, so that it will fit into a casserole. Heat the butter and oil in a flameproof casserole, add the pheasant and fry until browned all over.
2. Remove from the pot. Add the onion and bacon to the casserole and fry until lightly coloured. Add the apples, apple juice, salt and pepper.
3. Place the pheasant on top. Cover the casserole and cook in a preheated oven for about 1¼ hours or until the breast is tender. Lift out the pheasant and cut into quarters. Cool.
To Freeze: Pack the pheasant portions into a rigid container and cover. Pack the vegetable mixture in a separate container. Freeze both.
To Serve: Allow to thaw at room temperature for 3-4 hours. Put the pheasant portions into a roasting tin, cover with foil and reheat in a preheated oven (180°C, 350°F, Gas Mark 4) for about 40 minutes or until heated through. Meanwhile, coat the apple rings in the sugar and fry in the butter until browned. Keep hot. Place the vegetable mixture in a saucepan and bring slowly to boil, stirring occasionally. Simmer until reduced by a third. Add the Calvados, set alight and shake the pan until the flames die down. Stir in the cream, and taste and adjust the seasoning. Heat, but do not boil. Serve the pheasant with the sauce poured over and garnished with the apple rings.

GUINEA FOWL WITH GRAPES

2 young oven-ready guinea fowl, about 450 g/1 lb each, with giblets
1 small onion
½ teaspoon dried thyme
salt
freshly ground black pepper
4 streaky bacon rashers, rind removed
350 g (12 oz) black grapes
2 tablespoons plain flour
To serve:
2 slices of bread, crusts removed, quartered diagonally
oil for frying
75 g (3 oz) black grapes, halved and seeded

Preparation time: 15-60 minutes
Cooking time: 1¾-2 hours
Oven: 160°C, 325°F, Gas Mark 3

1. Remove the giblets from the birds, put them into a saucepan with the onion, thyme and water to cover. Add salt and pepper. Bring to the boil and simmer for 30 minutes. Strain and reserve 150 ml (¼ pint) of the stock.
2. Cover each guinea fowl with 2 rashers of bacon (if the birds are already larded remove the plain fat). Put the birds into a deep casserole, side by side.
3. Pack the grapes all round the birds. Cover with a tight-fitting lid or foil.
4. Cook in a preheated oven for 1¾-2 hours or until the birds feel well cooked and tender when pierced through the breast with a pointed knife.
5. Lift out the guinea fowl. Rub the grapes and liquid through a strainer into a saucepan.
6. Blend the flour with the reserved giblet stock, stir into the grape purée and bring to the boil, stirring until thickened. Add salt and pepper. Cool.
To Freeze: Put the guinea fowl and sauce into separate rigid containers, cover and freeze.
To Serve: Allow to thaw in the refrigerator for 6-8 hours. Put the birds into a roasting tin, cover with foil and reheat in a preheated oven (190°C, 375°F, Gas Mark 5) for about 45 minutes. Meanwhile, place the sauce in a pan and bring slowly to the boil, stirring occasionally. Taste and adjust the seasoning. Fry the bread triangles in oil until golden brown. Remove the bacon from the guinea fowl, cut the birds in half and serve with some sauce poured over them. Garnish with the croûtons and halved grapes. Serve the remaining sauce separately.

FROM THE TOP: Pigeon and steak pie; Pheasant with apples and cream; Guinea fowl with grapes

INDIVIDUAL BEEF WELLINGTONS

4 fillet steaks, about 175 g (6 oz) each
a little oil
1 garlic clove, peeled and crushed
100 g (4 oz) soft liver pâté
1 x 375 g (13 oz) packet frozen puff pastry, thawed
beaten egg, to glaze

Preparation time: 20 minutes
Cooking time: 20-25 minutes
Oven: 220°C, 425°F, Gas Mark 7

1. If necessary, trim any fat from the steaks. Brush the steaks with oil and cook under a preheated high grill to seal both sides. Reduce the heat to medium and cook for a further 3 minutes on each side. Cool.

2. Mix the garlic into the pâté.

3. Roll out the pastry dough thinly and cut into 4 rectangles large enough to enclose a steak.

4. Put a steak into the centre of each rectangle. Spread the steaks with the pâté. Dampen the edges of the pastry and fold over the sides and ends. Tuck underneath and seal. Decorate with pastry leaves cut from the trimmings.

To Freeze: Open freeze on a baking sheet. When solid, wrap in freezer film and foil and return to the freezer.

To Serve: Allow to thaw in the refrigerator for 4-6 hours. Unwrap and put on a baking sheet. Brush with beaten egg and bake in a preheated oven for 20-25 minutes or until well risen and golden brown. Serve hot with vegetables.

FROM THE LEFT: Individual beef Wellingtons; Beef steaks chasseur

BEEF STEAKS CHASSEUR

Serves 6
50 g (2 oz) butter
2 tablespoons oil
1 large onion, peeled, halved and finely sliced
450 g (1 lb) mushrooms, finely chopped
150 ml (¼ pint) white wine
2 beef stock cubes
salt
freshly ground black pepper
6 x 200 g (7 oz) sirloin or porterhouse steaks, cut at least 2.5 cm (1 inch) thick
parsley sprigs, to garnish

Preparation time: 25 minutes
Cooking time: 30-45 minutes
Oven: 200°C, 400°F, Gas Mark 6

For this recipe buy thick steaks that after cooking will be juicy and still slightly pink in the centre.

1. Heat the butter and oil in a frying pan, add the onion and fry gently until transparent but not coloured. Add the mushrooms and cook gently until softened, about 8-10 minutes.
2. Stir in the wine, crumbled stock cubes, and salt and pepper and cook for a further 5 minutes.
3. Meanwhile, cook the steaks under a preheated high grill to seal, about 4 minutes on each side. Cool.
To Freeze: Put each steak on a sheet of foil and spread the mushroom mixture evenly over the top. Wrap up and seal as individual parcels. Freeze.
To Serve: Allow to thaw at room temperature for 3-4 hours. Place the parcels on a baking sheet and cook in a preheated oven for 30-45 minutes, according to how well done you like the steaks. Serve garnished with parsley.

HOT BEEF GALANTINE

Serves 6
750 g (1½ lb) rump steak
225 g (8 oz) lean cooked ham
1 large onion, peeled
75 g (3 oz) fresh brown breadcrumbs
2 eggs
1 teaspoon dried mixed herbs
1 tablespoon chopped parsley
2 teaspoons salt
freshly ground black pepper
Topping:
2 large beef tomatoes, skinned and chopped
1 x 200 g (7 oz) can pimentos, well drained and chopped
1 medium onion, peeled and finely sliced

Preparation time: 25 minutes
Cooking time: 1½ hours
Oven: 180°C, 350°F, Gas Mark 4

This is a very versatile recipe which is just as good served cold for a buffet. Thaw overnight in the refrigerator, turn out and sprinkle with chopped parsley and chives. Serve on a bed of shredded lettuce with salads and hot brown bread.

1. Mince the steak, ham and onion, then mix with the breadcrumbs, eggs, herbs, parsley, salt and pepper.
2. To make the topping, put the ingredients into a saucepan and cook gently for 10 minutes until softened, stirring occasionally.
3. Spread the topping over the bottom of a 1.5 kg (3 lb) non-stick loaf tin. Cover with the meat mixture, spreading evenly. Cover with greaseproof paper and foil.
4. Stand the tin in a roasting tin containing about 2.5 cm (1 inch) of water. Cook in a preheated oven for 1½ hours. Cool.
To Freeze: Cover with fresh greaseproof peper and foil and freeze.
To Serve: Allow to thaw at room temperature for 3-4 hours. Return the covered loaf tin to the roasting tin containing water and cook in a preheated oven for about 1 hour. Turn out and serve with duchesse potatoes and green vegetables.

Variation:
For **Pâté en Croûte**, take 450 g (1 lb) short crust pastry and use 350 g (12 oz) to line the loaf tin. Fill with the minced meat mixture, cover with the remaining pastry, brush with beaten egg and bake at 200°C, 400°F, Gas Mark 6 for 30 minutes. Reduce the heat to 170°C, 325°F, Gas Mark 3 for a further 45 minutes. Allow to cool. Turn out, wrap as above and freeze. Thaw overnight and serve warmed or cold with the tomato and pepper sauce. Do not refreeze.

TOPSIDE POT ROAST

Serves 6
2 tablespoons oil
2 large leeks, cut into 1 cm (½ inch) rings
3 celery sticks, sliced
1 tablespoon tomato purée
300 ml (½ pint) light ale
salt
freshly ground black pepper
1.25 kg (2½ lb) joint of topside of beef
2 tablespoons plain flour
To serve:
2 large leeks, cut into 1 cm (½ inch) rings
3 celery sticks, sliced
25 g (1 oz) butter
celery leaves, to garnish

Preparation time: 20 minutes
Cooking time: 2 hours
Oven: 160°C, 325°F, Gas Mark 3

For a family meal use this same recipe for a boned and rolled brisket, which is cheaper. It will need about another 30-45 minutes cooking time.

1. Heat the oil in a frying pan, add the leeks and celery and fry until lightly coloured. Put into the bottom of a deep casserole.
2. Stir together the tomato purée and 150 ml (½ pint) of the ale. Add to the vegetables with the salt and pepper.
3. Place the joint of beef on top. Cover the casserole and cook in a preheated oven for about 2 hours or until the meat is tender.
4. Lift out the joint. Cool a little, then cut into about 12 slices. Drain the vegetables, reserving the liquid. Skim off the excess fat. Make up the liquid to 150 ml (¼ pint) with water.
5. Blend the flour with the remaining ale in a saucepan. Stir in the reserved cooking liquid and cook until thickened.
To Freeze: Spread the vegetables in a rigid freezer container, lay the meat slices, overlapping, on top and cover. Pack the sauce in a separate rigid container. Freeze both.
To Serve: Allow to thaw at room temperature for 3-4 hours. Put the meat and vegetables into an ovenproof serving dish. Cover and reheat in a preheated oven (160°C, 325°F, Gas Mark 3) for about 30 minutes or until heated through. Meanwhile, cook the leeks and celery in the butter until softened, about 10 minutes. Put the sauce into a pan and slowly bring to the boil, stirring occasionally. Pour over the meat. Serve with the vegetables and garnish with celery leaves.

ABOVE: Hot beef galantine; BELOW: Topside pot roast

PORK AND SAGE GOUJONS

Serves 6
175 g (6 oz) fresh white breadcrumbs
4 teaspoons dried sage
1 teaspoon salt
freshly ground black pepper
2 x 275 g (10 oz) pork fillets
2 eggs, beaten
oil for deep frying

Preparation time: 30 minutes
Cooking time: 30 minutes

These are very good for a dinner party, served with Lyonnaise potatoes and broccoli.

1. Mix together the breadcrumbs, sage and salt and pepper.
2. Cut the pork into thin strips about 7.5 cm (3 inches) long and 5 mm (¼ inch) thick.
3. Dip the strips into the egg, then coat evenly in the crumb mixture. Place the strips in a single layer on a baking sheet.
To Freeze: Open freeze. When solid, pack in a freezer container or bag, cover and return to the freezer.
To Serve: Deep fry from frozen in oil heated to 190°C/ 375°F, (when a cube of bread bubbles and instantly rises to the surface), for 5-8 minutes or until browned, crisp and cooked through. Drain on paper towels and serve with a sauce of apples cooked in cider, sweetened to taste.

PORK LOIN STUFFED WITH ORANGE AND ONION

Serves 6
Stuffing:
25 g (1 oz) butter
1 large onion, peeled and thinly sliced
grated rind and chopped flesh of 2 large oranges
4 digestive biscuits, crushed
salt
freshly ground black pepper
1.5 kg (3 lb) loin of pork, boned and rind removed
a little oil
1 tablespoon brown sugar
¼ teaspoon ground coriander
To garnish:
orange slices
lettuce hearts
watercress

Preparation time: 20 minutes
Cooking time: 1¾-2 hours
Oven: 180°C, 350°F, Gas Mark 4

The pork rind is removed to facilitate carving. For extra crisp crackling, roast the rind separately.

1. To make the stuffing, melt the butter in a frying pan, add the onion and fry until lightly coloured. Stir in the orange rind and flesh, biscuit crumbs and salt and pepper.
2. Lay the meat flat and spread over the stuffing. Roll up and tie with string. Score the fat diagonally into diamond patterns.
3. Put the meat into a roasting tin. Rub the fat with oil, then rub in the sugar, coriander, and salt and pepper.
4. Roast in a preheated oven for 1¾-2 hours or until cooked and golden. Test with a skewer – if the juices run pink, cook for a further 10-15 minutes. Cool.
To Freeze: Wrap in freezer film and foil, or put into a container and cover. Freeze.
To Serve: Allow to thaw in the refrigerator for 12 hours. To serve cold, slice the meat and arrange on a serving dish. Garnish with peeled sliced oranges, lettuce hearts and watercress. Serve with salads or pickles and baked jacket potatoes. To serve hot, replace in the roasting tin, brush with a little oil and reheat in a preheated oven (180°C, 350°F, Gas Mark 4) for about 45 minutes. Serve, sliced, with vegetables and gravy made with the pan juices and 2-3 tablespoons fresh orange juice.

DEVILLED PORK CHOPS

Serves 6
6 large pork chops
a little oil
salt
freshly ground black pepper
1 x 225 g (8 oz) can tomatoes
3 tablespoons tomato ketchup
1 tablespoon soy sauce
2 tablespoons Worcestershire sauce
2 teaspoons French mustard
2 tablespoons wine vinegar
1 tablespoon brown sugar
250 g (9 oz) long-grain rice, to serve

Preparation time: 10 minutes
Cooking time: 20 minutes
Oven: 180°C, 350°F, Gas Mark 4

This dish has a real bite to it, so serve with plain rice (which can have the ginger added or not as you prefer). You need to know your guests like spicy food before you serve this at a dinner party! Choose loin chops without kidney or substitute spare-rib chops which have very little bone. These may need slightly longer cooking.

1. Put the chops in a grill pan, brush with oil and sprinkle with salt and pepper. Cook under a preheated medium grill until browned on both sides, about 20 minutes. Cool.
2. Purée the tomatoes with the liquid in a blender or food processor. Mix with the ketchup, the sauces, mustard, vinegar and sugar.
To Freeze: Put the chops into a rigid container, pour the tomato sauce over and cover. Freeze.
To Serve: Allow to thaw at room temperature for 3-4 hours. Place the chops and sauce in an oven-proof serving dish. Cover and cook in a preheated oven for about 45 minutes or until heated through and bubbling. Serve the chops with rice cooked in boiling salted water with a bay leaf. To give extra flavour to the rice, add a 2.5 cm (1 inch) piece of fresh root ginger, peeled and finely chopped, to the water.

Variation:
Use apples and redcurrants for a fruity, rather than a spicy sauce. Put 300 ml/½ pint unsweetened apple juice, 3 tablespoons redcurrant jelly, and ½ teaspoon dried or 1 teaspoon finely chopped fresh sage in a pan. Warm gently, stirring, until the jelly dissolves. Simmer for 2-3 minutes to thicken the sauce slightly. Pour over the cooked chops and freeze and serve as above.

Pork and sage goujons; Pork loin stuffed with orange and onion

VEAL ESCALOPES WITH MUSHROOMS MARSALA

2 tablespoons plain flour
salt
freshly ground black pepper
grated rind of 1 small orange
4 veal escalopes, beaten until thin
75 g (3 oz) butter
1 tablespoon oil
225 g (8 oz) tight button mushrooms, finely sliced
To serve:
150 ml (¼ pint) Marsala
4 tablespoons soured cream

Preparation time: 10 minutes
Cooking time: 10-12 minutes
Oven: 180°C, 350°F, Gas Mark 4

Veal is not readily available everywhere and is also seasonal. Turkey fillets are a good substitute. Sweet sherry could be used instead of Marsala.

1. Mix together the flour, salt and pepper and orange rind and use to coat the escalopes.
2. Heat 50 g (2 oz) of the butter with the oil in a frying pan. Add the escalopes and cook over a gentle heat for about 4 minutes on each side.
3. Remove from the pan and set aside to cool. Add the rest of the butter to the pan, allow to melt, then fry the mushrooms for 3 minutes, turning gently. Cool.
To Freeze: Put the escalopes into a rigid freezer container with the mushrooms on top, cover and freeze.
To Serve: Allow to thaw at room temperature for 4-6 hours. Put the escalopes, with the mushrooms on top, into an ovenproof serving dish. Pour over the Marsala, cover and heat in a preheated oven for 25-30 minutes or until heated through. Trickle the soured cream on top and serve with courgettes, boiled and tossed in butter.

Variation:
Veal Grand Marnier: Omit the mushrooms and add 2 teaspoons dried tarragon. Use 2 large oranges instead of 1 small one and 2 tablespoons Grand Marnier. Mix the tarragon with the flour as in step 1, omitting the orange rind. Fry the escalopes as in step 2. Add the rest of the butter to the pan with the grated rind of both oranges and the juice of one. Bring to the boil, stirring to incorporate the pan juices. Remove the pith from the second orange and cut into segments. Add to the pan together with the Grand Marnier. Bring back to the boil, taste and adjust the seasoning. Add a little water if necessary to thin the sauce. Serve the escalopes topped with a spoonful of the orange sauce.

VEAL AND HAM RAISED PIE

Serves 10
Pastry:
350 g (12 oz) plain flour
1 teaspoon salt
1 egg yolk
100 g (4 oz) lard
150 ml (¼ pint) water
Filling:
450 g (1 lb) pie veal, diced
2 tablespoons chopped parsley
2 tablespoons chopped chives
1 teaspoon dried thyme
grated rind of ½ lemon
350 g (12 oz) lean green boiling bacon, soaked, drained
   and diced
salt
freshly ground black pepper
beaten egg, to glaze
about 600 ml (1 pint) veal bone stock

Preparation time: 40 minutes
Cooking time: 3¼-3½ hours
Oven: 230°C, 450°F, Gas Mark 8;
      160°C, 325°F, Gas Mark 3

Raised pastry is so good for this kind of pie and it is easier to make than you may think. This recipe uses a round, loose-bottomed cake tin, but you could make it in a 1 kg (2 lb) loaf tin if preferred.

1. Sift the flour and salt into a bowl. Add the egg yolk. Place the lard and water in a saucepan and slowly bring to the boil. Pour immediately on to the flour and mix quickly to a soft dough. Cover and keep warm while assembling the pie.
2. Using three-quarters of the dough, line a round 20 cm (8 inch) loose-bottomed cake tin, moulding the dough up the sides of the tin evenly with the hands.
3. Fill with alternate layers of veal, herbs, lemon rind and bacon, seasoning each layer with salt and pepper.
4. Roll out the remaining dough to make a lid. Dampen the edges and seal by pinching them together. Mark the top of the pie into 10 portions with a knife. Brush well with beaten egg.
5. Bake in a preheated oven for 20 minutes, then reduce the heat and bake for a further 3 hours. After 2 hours cover the top with foil if it is becoming too brown.
6. Cool the pie in the tin. When cold, cut out one section of the top pastry with a small sharp knife. Pour in the veal stock until the pie is filled. Replace the pastry and chill the pie.
To Freeze: Remove the pie from the tin. Wrap in foil and freeze.
To Serve: Allow to thaw at room temperature for 12 hours. Serve sliced with salads or pickles.

CLOCKWISE FROM THE TOP: Kidneys in brandy cream with noodles; Veal and ham raised pie; Veal escalopes with mushrooms Marsala

KIDNEYS IN BRANDY CREAM WITH NOODLES

100 g (4 oz) butter
1 shallot, peeled and finely chopped
450 g (1 lb) lambs' kidneys, quartered and cored
100 g (4 oz) button mushrooms, quartered
salt
freshly ground black pepper
To serve:
225 g (8 oz) egg noodles
25 g (1 oz) butter
6 tablespoons brandy, warmed
300 ml (½ pint) double cream
chopped parsley, to garnish

Preparation time: 15 minutes
Cooking time: 10 minutes

1. Melt the butter in a frying pan, add the shallot and fry gently until softened. Add the kidneys and cook for 5 minutes.
2. Add the mushrooms and cook for a further 5 minutes. Add salt and pepper and cool.
To Freeze: Put into a rigid freezer container, cover and freeze.
To Serve: Allow to thaw at room temperature for 4-6 hours. Place in a saucepan and slowly bring to the boil, stirring occasionally. Meanwhile, cook the noodles in boiling salted water for 8-10 minutes or until just tender. Drain and toss with the butter. Pour the warmed brandy over the kidneys, set alight and then add the cream. Heat until hot but not boiling. Taste and adjust the seasoning. Serve on the noodles, sprinkled with chopped parsley.

SPANISH PAËLLA

4 fresh squid, about 350 g (12 oz)
4 tablespoons olive oil
225 g (8 oz) skinless chicken meat, cubed
100 g (4 oz) lean boneless pork, cubed
1 medium onion, peeled and chopped
1 garlic clove, peeled and crushed
225 g (8 oz) tomatoes, skinned, seeded and quartered
350 g (12 oz) long-grain rice
4 pinches of saffron threads, or 1 teaspoon turmeric
900 ml (1½ pints) hot chicken stock
2 teaspoons salt
freshly ground black pepper
To serve:
about 600 ml (1 pint) fresh mussels, well scrubbed
100 g (4 oz) frozen cooked peeled prawns, thawed
1 red pepper, cored, seeded and sliced
8 pimento-stuffed green olives, halved
100 g (4 oz) frozen peas
8 frozen large prawns, cooked but not shelled, and thawed
lemon wedges

Preparation time: 45 minutes
Cooking time: 25-30 minutes

This traditional Spanish recipe is normally cooked and served in a paëlla pan but you can use a deep frying pan and serve on a large platter.

1. Prepare the squid and cut the sac into rings about 5 mm (¼ inch) wide.
2. Heat the oil in a large pan or deep frying pan, add the chicken and pork cubes and fry until sealed and evenly browned. Add the onion and garlic and cook for a further 5 minutes.
3. Stir in the squid, tomatoes and rice and cook for 5 minutes. Meanwhile, soak the saffron threads in the hot stock for 5 minutes. Strain and add the stock to the pan (or mix the turmeric with the stock). Add salt and pepper. Cover with a lid or foil and cook on a very low heat for about 15 minutes, stirring occasionally, until the rice is tender and the liquid nearly absorbed. Cool.
To Freeze: Put into a rigid freezer container, cover and freeze.
To Serve: Allow to thaw in the refrigerator for 12 hours. Put into a large pan and reheat gently, stirring occasionally until very hot. To prepare the mussels, scrape off the 'beards' and discard any mussels that are open or broken. Steam, covered, in 300 ml (½ pint) boiling water for 5 minutes, shaking the pan occasionally, until the shells open. Discard any mussels that do not open. Keep hot. Add the peeled prawns, red pepper, olives and peas to the paëlla and cook for a further 5 minutes, covered. Serve with the mussels and large prawns and lemon wedges arranged on top.

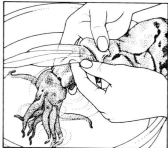
Remove the bone from the sac.

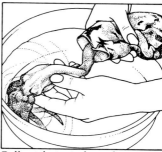
Pull out the tentacles and guts.

Peel away the patchy skin.

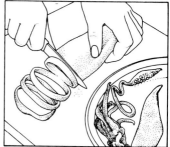
Cut the body sac into rings.

FILLETS OF SOLE PRINCESS

1 x 350 g (12 oz) can asparagus spears, drained
4 Dover sole fillets, about 750 g (1½ lb), skinned
50 g (2 oz) butter
1 shallot, peeled and finely chopped
5 tablespoons dry white wine
5 tablespoons well seasoned fish stock
150 ml (¼ pint) double cream
salt
freshly ground white pepper

Preparation time: 10 minutes
Cooking time: 20 minutes
Oven: 180°C, 350°F, Gas Mark 4

Ask the fishmonger for the bones and skin of the sole so that you can make a fish stock. Boil them as you would giblets with a little parsley, pared lemon rind and salt and pepper. Strain.

1. Reserve 8 asparagus spears for the garnish and chop the rest.
2. Lay the sole fillets, skinned side up, on a board. Divide the chopped asparagus between them and fold each fillet into 3.
3. Butter an ovenproof dish with 25 g (1 oz) of the butter. Sprinkle with the shallot and lay the fish on top. Pour over the wine and fish stock. Cover with foil and cook in a preheated oven for about 15 minutes.
4. Lift the fish fillets into a rigid freezer container. Pour the stock into a saucepan and boil to reduce by half, then remove the pan from the heat. Add the rest of the butter, shaking the pan to incorporate it into the stock.
5. Whip the cream lightly and fold in. Taste and adjust for seasoning. Pour over the fish. Cool.
To Freeze: Cover and freeze. Freeze the reserved spears separately, wrapped in foil.
To Serve: Allow to thaw in the refrigerator for 6-8 hours. Transfer the fish and sauce to an oven-proof serving dish, cover and heat in a preheated oven for about 20 minutes. Warm the reserved asparagus spears in a little water and drain. Glaze the top of the fish under a preheated hot grill for 2 minutes, then garnish with the asparagus spears and serve with whirls of piped mashed potato and French beans.

FRESH SALMON MOUSSE

350 g (12 oz) tail piece of fresh salmon
½ teaspoon dill seeds
salt
freshly ground black pepper
1 lemon
3 tablespoons water
15 g (½ oz) gelatine
100 g (4 oz) rich full-fat soft cheese
150 ml (¼ pint) thick mayonnaise
150 ml (¼ pint) plain unsweetened yogurt
1 large dill cucumber, finely chopped
To garnish:
1 hard-boiled egg, separated
pimento-stuffed green olives, sliced
chopped parsley

Preparation time: 30 minutes, plus chilling
Cooking time: 5 minutes

1. Put the fish in a saucepan with the dill seeds, salt and pepper. Pare the rind thinly from half the lemon and add to the pan. Cover with cold water and bring to the boil. Simmer for 5 minutes. Leave to cool in the pan for 15 minutes, then drain the fish and discard the flavourings.
2. Remove the skin and bones from the fish and mash the flesh well.
3. Put the measured water in a cup, sprinkle over the gelatine and leave to soak for 5 minutes or until spongy. Stand the cup in a pan of hot water and stir until the gelatine has completely dissolved.
4. Whisk together the cheese, mayonnaise and yogurt until smooth.
5. Add the fish, gelatine mixture and dill cucumber, and mix well. Finely grate the rind from the rest of the lemon and add to the mixture.
6. Put into a 450 g (1 lb) loaf tin, cover with freezer film and foil and chill until set.
To Freeze: Freeze. When frozen, turn out of the tin, wrap in freezer film and foil and return to the freezer.
To Serve: Unwrap and put on a serving plate. Allow to thaw in the refrigerator for 4-6 hours. Finely chop the hard-boiled egg white and sieve the yolk. Arrange the egg white, yolk, olives and parsley in diagonal stripes across the top of the mousse repeating each coloured stripe once. Serve with crisp shredded lettuce, cucumber in plain unsweetened yogurt with chives, and boiled new potatoes.

Fresh salmon mousse; Seafood salads

SEAFOOD SALADS

4 large scallops, fresh or frozen
1 bay leaf
4 strips of pared lemon rind
salt
freshly ground black pepper
3 tablespoons water
15 g (½ oz) gelatine
50 g (2 oz) long-grain rice, cooked and cooled
100 g (4 oz) cooked peeled prawns
1 tablespoon chopped parsley
1 tablespoon lemon juice
25 g (1 oz) flaked almonds
2 celery sticks, finely sliced
6 tablespoons thick mayonnaise
4 cleaned scallop shells

To serve:
4 tablespoons mayonnaise
unpeeled prawns
4 parsley sprigs
paprika

Preparation time: 30 minutes
Cooking time: 10 minutes

1. Place the scallops in a saucepan with the bay leaf, lemon rind, salt and pepper. Cover with water, bring to the boil and poach for 10 minutes. Drain, discarding the flavourings, and chop. Cool.
2. Put the measured water in a cup, sprinkle over the gelatine and soak for 5 minutes until spongy. Stand the cup in hot water and stir until the gelatine has completely dissolved.
3. Add the gelatine to the scallops with the rice, prawns, parsley, lemon juice, almonds, celery and mayonnaise. Taste and adjust the seasoning. Fill the scallop shells with the mixture.
4. Chill until set.
To Freeze: Wrap each shell in freezer film and foil and freeze.
To Serve: Allow to thaw in the refrigerator for 6-8 hours. Serve in the shells, topped with mayonnaise, a whole prawn, a parsley sprig and a little paprika. Put on a bed of lettuce and serve with hot rolls.

PUDDINGS

STRAWBERRY AND ORANGE GÂTEAU

Serves 6
3 eggs
75 g (3 oz) caster sugar, warmed
75 g (3 oz) self-raising flour
1 tablespoon hot water
Buttercream:
100 g (4 oz) butter, softened
225 g (8 oz) icing sugar, sifted
grated rind of 1 orange
2 tablespoons orange juice
To serve:
150 ml (¼ pint) double cream
225 g (8 oz) fresh or frozen strawberries
2-3 tablespoons redcurrant jelly, melted

Preparation time: 30 minutes
Cooking time: 10 minutes
Oven: 220°C, 425°F, Gas Mark 7

1. Grease and line a 28 x 18 cm (11 x 7 inch) Swiss roll tin.
2. Break the eggs into a bowl. Add the sugar and whisk until thick, pale and the whisk leaves a trail when lifted.
3. Sift the flour over the whisked mixture and fold in with a metal spoon. Add the hot water.
4. Spoon the mixture into the prepared tin and spread evenly. Bake in a preheated oven for 10 minutes or until risen, golden and springy to touch.
5. Turn out on to a sheet of non-stick silicone paper. Leave the lining paper on the cake, cover with a damp tea towel and leave to cool.
6. Beat together the butter, icing sugar, orange rind and juice until blended, smooth and soft.
7. Remove the towel and paper from the sponge. Trim the crusty edges from the sides of the sponge, then cut into four equal strips lengthways. Spread each strip with the buttercream.
8. Take one strip of sponge, stand it on its edge and curl it round into a spiral with the iced side in. Join the next strip of sponge to the end of the first and continue to wind round, using the remaining strips to complete the spiral.
To Freeze: Open freeze, then wrap and store.
To Serve: Allow to thaw for 2 hours in the refrigerator. Whip the cream and spread half over the side of the cake. Cover the top with the strawberries (thawed if frozen) and brush with the melted redcurrant jelly to glaze. Pipe the top decoratively with the remaining cream. Serve chilled, cut into wedges.

LIME CHEESECAKE

Serves 4-6
Base:
75 g (3 oz) digestive biscuits, finely crushed
40 g (1½ oz) butter, melted
25 g (1 oz) demerara sugar
Filling:
1 x 600 ml (1 pint) lime jelly tablet
grated rind and juice of 1 lime
225 g (8 oz) cottage cheese, sieved
150 ml (¼ pint) double cream
1 tablespoon caster sugar
To decorate:
double or whipping cream, whipped
candied angelica leaves

Preparation time: 25 minutes, plus cooling and chilling

This is a very light cheesecake because of the jelly and cottage cheese. For a special occasion a richer version could be made using full fat soft cheese.

1. Mix together the biscuit crumbs, butter and sugar. Press evenly over the bottom of an 18 cm (7 inch) diameter flan tin or ring standing on a baking sheet. Chill.
2. To make the filling, make up the jelly to 300 ml (½ pint) with boiling water. Stir until completely dissolved. Add the lime rind and juice. Chill until nearly set.
3. Mix the cottage cheese with the cream. Stir in the jelly and sugar until smooth and well blended. (This could be done in a blender.)
4. Pour into the flan tin and chill until set.
5. Pipe the whipped cream for the decoration in rosettes on a flat sheet.
To Freeze: Open freeze the rosettes and cheesecake. Put the frozen cream rosettes into a rigid freezer container and cover. When the cheesecake is solid, wrap it. Freeze both.
To Serve: Allow the cheesecake to thaw in the refrigerator for 4 hours. Place the rosettes on top and thaw for a further 2 hours. Decorate with angelica leaves and serve chilled.

ORANGES AND GRAPEFRUIT WITH CARAMEL SAUCE

4 large oranges, preferably navel
2 grapefruit
Sauce:
100 g (4 oz) sugar
600 ml (1 pint) water

Preparation time: 10 minutes
Cooking time: about 15 minutes

This is best made when 'navel' oranges are available as they have no pips. Make variations by using tangerines, satsumas, uglis and the rosy grapefruit.

1. Pare the rind thinly from the oranges and grapefruit. Cut the rind into thin strips and blanch in boiling water for 1 minute. Drain.
2. With a sharp knife, cut all the white pith from the oranges and grapefruit. Cut the fruit into slices. or carefully remove each segment.
3. Put the sugar and 450 ml (¾ pint) of the water into a heavy saucepan. Heat gently, without stirring, until the sugar has dissolved. Boil rapidly until the syrup turns a rich golden colour.
4. Cover your hands with oven gloves, then take the pan off the heat and pour in the rest of the water. Swirl around to mix to a smooth syrup. If lumps of caramel form, reheat gently until they melt.
To Freeze: Put the fruit into a rigid freezer container. Cover and freeze. Freeze the strips of rind and sauce separately.
To Serve: Allow to thaw in the refrigerator for 6 hours. Arrange the fruit slices alternately on a shallow serving dish, decorate with the strips of rind and pour over a little sauce. Serve the rest of the sauce separately.

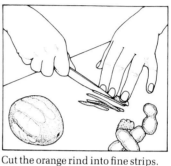 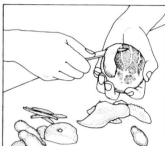

Cut the orange rind into fine strips.   Cut away the pith and slice.

BLACKBERRY AND APPLE TANSY

Serves 6
40 g (1½ oz) butter
225 g (8 oz) cooking apples, peeled, cored and sliced
225 g (8 oz) blackberries
75 g (3 oz) sugar
2 tablespoons ground rice
grated rind of 1 lemon
1 egg, separated
150 ml (¼ pint) double cream, lightly whipped, to serve

Preparation time: 15 minutes, plus cooling
Cooking time: 10 minutes

Tansy is an old-fashioned herb with a rather bitter taste. Easter cakes were flavoured with it and eaten on Good Friday as a reminder of the Passion. It was also used to flavour fruit puddings; nowadays we use the sharpness of lemon instead, while keeping the old name for the dish. This pudding can also be made with damsons or blackcurrants.

1. Melt the butter in a saucepan. Add the apples and cook gently until soft but not coloured. Add the blackberries and cook until tender.
2. Sieve the fruit. Return the purée to the saucepan and stir in the sugar, ground rice and lemon rind. Beat in the egg yolk and cook very gently, stirring, for about 5 minutes or until thickened. Cool.
To Freeze: Put into a rigid freezer container, cover and freeze. Pack and freeze the egg white separately.
To Serve: Allow the purée and egg white to thaw in the refrigerator for 6 hours. Put the purée into individual dishes. Whisk the egg white until stiff, fold into the cream and spoon on top of the purée. Serve chilled.

GINGER CREAM

Serves 6
150 ml (¼ pint) whipping cream, lightly whipped
300 ml (½ pint) plain unsweetened yogurt
75 g (3 oz) ginger nut biscuits, finely crushed
25 g (1 oz) crystallized or stem ginger, chopped
To serve:
12 pieces of crystallized or stem ginger
chocolate fingers or langue de chat biscuits

Preparation time: 15 minutes

CHOCOLATE AND CHESTNUT TEMPTATION

Serves 6
100 g (4 oz) plain chocolate
75 g (3 oz) butter, softened
40 g (1½ oz) caster sugar
1 x 200 g (7 oz) can unsweetened chestnut purée
50 g (2 oz) plain sweet biscuits, broken into 1 cm (½ inch) square pieces
40 g (1½ oz) glacé cherries, chopped

Preparation time: 15 minutes

This pudding is quite tempting enough without any decoration, but for a special dinner party you could add piped rosettes of whipped cream, topped with pieces of marron glacé.

1. Break the chocolate into a heatproof basin and place it over a pan of hot water, over a gentle heat. Stir until the chocolate has melted.
2. Cream the butter and sugar together until light and fluffy. Beat in the chestnut purée and chocolate until smooth. Fold in the biscuits and cherries.
3. Line an 18 cm (7 inch) round sponge tin with greaseproof paper. Pour in the mixture and spread out evenly. Make swirled patterns on top with a knife.
To Freeze: Cover and freeze.
To Serve: Run a warmed knife around the edge of the cake to loosen it from the tin and warm the base of the tin with your hands. Turn out the cake on to a serving plate. Peel off the greaseproof paper. Allow to thaw in the refrigerator for about 1 hour before serving, cut into wedges.

1. Stir together the cream, yogurt and biscuits, then fold in the ginger.
To Freeze: Put into a rigid freezer container, cover and freeze.
To Serve: Allow to thaw in the refrigerator for 6 hours. Stir and spoon into individual glasses. Top each serving with two pieces of ginger and serve with biscuits.

Oranges and grapefruit with caramel sauce; Blackberry and apple tansy

BRANDIED FRUITS ICE CREAM

25 g (1 oz) dried apricots
1 x 5 cm (2 inch) square piece of candied angelica
25 g (1 oz) maraschino cherries, chopped
25 g (1 oz) seedless raisins
25 g (1 oz) chopped mixed candied peel
15 g (½ oz) flaked almonds
1 tablespoon maraschino syrup
2 tablespoons brandy
Basic ice cream mixture:
2 eggs, separated
50 g (2 oz) caster sugar
150 ml (¼ pint) double cream

Preparation time: 25 minutes, plus soaking and freezing

This ice cream is very easy to make and does not need stirring during freezing. You might like to make a double quantity and divide it into two different flavours. The addition of alcohol makes a softer ice cream which can be scooped straight from the freezer. However, the fruit purée ice cream, described in the variations, needs thawing in the refrigerator for about 1 hour before serving.

1. Soak the apricots and angelica in boiling water for 10 minutes. Drain and chop.
2. Mix together all the fruits, the peel and the almonds in a bowl. Add the maraschino syrup and brandy, stir and leave to soak for 6 hours, stirring the mixture occasionally.
3. Whisk the egg whites until they form soft peaks. Beat in the sugar gradually and continue beating until the mixture is stiff and shiny.
4. Whip the cream until thick. Lightly beat the egg yolks. Fold together the egg whites, cream and egg yolks until blended, then stir in the soaked fruits and their liquid.
To Freeze: Put into a rigid freezer container, cover and freeze for at least 6 hours.
To Serve: Serve scoops of ice cream in glasses. Accompany with wafers or biscuits if preferred.

Variations:
Rum and Blackcurrant Ice Cream: Cook 225 g (8 oz) blackcurrants with 50 g (2 oz) sugar until tender. Sieve and cool. Stir into the basic ice cream mixture, with 3 tablespoons rum. Freeze as above.
Mango Ice Cream: Purée 350 g (12 oz) fresh or canned mango and add to the basic ice cream mixture, with 4 tablespoons lemon juice. Freeze as above.

LEMON LAPIS PUDDING

Serves 4-6
3 egg whites
175 g (6 oz) caster sugar
Filling:
½ x 375 g (13 oz) can condensed milk
150 ml (¼ pint) double cream
finely grated rind and juice of 2 large lemons
To decorate:
double or whipping cream, whipped
quartered lemon slices
chopped roasted hazelnuts

Preparation time: 30 minutes
Cooking time: 1 hour
Oven: 150°C, 300°F, Gas Mark 2

Make double the quantity of filling (using the whole can of condensed milk) and freeze half to use in a trifle, to fill a flan case or to serve on its own.

1. Whisk the egg whites until they form soft peaks. Whisk in the sugar in three batches and continue whisking until the mixture is stiff and shiny.
2. Line baking sheets with non-stick silicone or lightly greased greaseproof paper and draw three 18 cm (7 inch) circles on the paper. Spread the meringue evenly inside the circles.
3. Put into a preheated oven and bake for 1 hour or until the meringue is lightly coloured and crisp. Leave to cool.
4. Put the condensed milk and cream in a bowl with the grated lemon rind. Whisk, adding the lemon juice gradually in a stream, until the mixture is thick.
To Freeze: Pack the meringue rounds into a rigid container, interleaving with foil. Cover with a tight-fitting lid. Pack the filling into a separate rigid freezer container. Freeze both.
To Serve: Allow the filling to thaw in the refrigerator for 6 hours. Thaw the meringue rounds at room temperature, separated and laid out on a flat surface. Peel the meringue rounds off the paper very carefully. Put one round on a serving plate, spread with half the lemon filling and place a second round on top. Spread with the remaining filling and top with the third meringue round. Decorate with rosettes of cream separated by lemon slices and sprinkled with hazelnuts. Serve the pudding chilled, cut into wedges. For a more special presentation, the top layer of meringue can be piped in a spiral.

> The surest way to make good meringue is to whisk in all the sugar. Whisk the egg whites until lightly stiff, add one third of the sugar and whisk in thoroughly. Repeat with the other two thirds, whisking well after each addition. Continue whisking until the mixture is stiff and shiny.

COFFEE ICE BUNS WITH HOT MOCHA SAUCE

Choux Pastry:
40 g (1½ oz) butter
150 ml (¼ pint) water
50 g (2 oz) plain flour, sifted
1 egg, beaten
coffee ice cream, for filling
Sauce:
25 g (1 oz) butter
2 tablespoons golden syrup
2 tablespoons cocoa powder
2 teaspoons instant coffee powder
3 tablespoons water

Preparation time: 25 minutes
Cooking time: 25-30 minutes
Oven: 200°C, 400°F, Gas Mark 6

The secret of choux pastry is to beat it really well but not for too long, otherwise the fat starts to separate. You may find it better to use an electric mixer if your arm is not strong! The sauce is quickly made just before serving so there is no need to freeze it.

1. To make the pastry, heat the butter and water gently in a saucepan until the butter has melted. Bring to the boil. Add all the flour immediately and beat until the dough is smooth and pulling away from the sides of the pan. If using a mixer, put the flour in the bowl, pour on the hot liquid and beat for about 1 minute. Cool for 3 minutes.
2. Add the egg in two batches, beating well to incorporate it.
3. Put the choux pastry into a piping bag fitted with a 1 cm (½ in) nozzle and pipe 8 buns on a lightly greased baking sheet. Alternatively, use two spoons to shape the buns.
4. Put into a preheated oven and bake for about 25 minutes or until risen, golden brown and firm. Make a small slit with a sharp pointed knife on one side of each bun and return them to the oven. Bake for 5 minutes longer. Cool on a wire tray.
To Freeze: Pack in a freezer bag.
To Serve: Allow the buns to thaw at room temperature for 30 minutes, then fill with spoonfuls of coffee ice cream and return to the freezer. To make the sauce, put all the ingredients into a small saucepan and heat, stirring, until blended. Bring to the boil and boil for 1 minute, then serve with the buns.

CLOCKWISE FROM THE TOP: Lemon lapis pudding; Coffee ice buns with hot mocha sauce; American apple cake

AMERICAN APPLE CAKE

225 g (8 oz) cooking apples, peeled, cored and diced
50 g (2 oz) sugar
75 g (3 oz) self-raising flour, sifted
½ teaspoon baking powder
¼ teaspoon salt
25 g (1 oz) hazelnuts, chopped
50 g (2 oz) seedless raisins
1 egg, beaten
¼ teaspoon vanilla essence
4 tablespoons cooking oil

Preparation time: 10 minutes
Cooking time: 1-1¼ hours
Oven: 180°C, 350°F, Gas Mark 4

This recipe can easily be doubled and made either in one large or two 900 ml (1½ pint) ovenproof dishes, then you could serve half as a hot pudding and the rest cold for afternoon tea the next day.

1. Put the apples, sugar, flour, baking powder, salt, nuts and raisins into a bowl.
2. Mix together the egg, vanilla essence and oil and add to the bowl. Stir until well blended.
3. Put into a lightly buttered 900 ml (1½ pint) ovenproof or foil dish. Spread out evenly.
To Freeze: Cover and freeze.
To Serve: Allow to thaw for 3 hours. Uncover and put into a preheated oven. Bake for 1-1¼ hours or until golden brown and slightly shrinking from the sides of the dish. Serve hot with cream or ice cream.

HOMELY BREAD PUDDING

Serves 4-6

150 g (5 oz) stale bread (2-3 days old), made into crumbs
25 g (1 oz) self-raising flour, sifted
50 g (2 oz) shredded suet
50 g (2 oz) dark soft brown sugar
1 teaspoon mixed spice
100 g (4 oz) mixed dried fruit
2 tablespoons chunky orange marmalade
1 egg, beaten
150 ml (¼ pint) milk

Preparation time: 15 minutes
Cooking time: 2 hours

Traditional Bread Pudding is normally baked. Although this recipe could be cooked in the same way, here it is steamed for a change.

1. Mix together all the ingredients until well blended.
2. Put into a buttered 900 ml (1½ pint) pudding basin.
To Freeze: Cover with buttered greaseproof paper and foil and seal well over the edge of the basin. Freeze.
To Serve: Allow to thaw in the refrigerator for 6 hours. Place the pudding basin in a pan of boiling water and steam for 2 hours. Turn out and serve hot with custard.

TREASURE ISLAND PUDDING

Serves 6
1 x 225 g (8 oz) can pineapple rings
100 g (4 oz) soft margarine
100 g (4 oz) caster sugar
100 g (4 oz) self-raising flour, sifted
25 g (1 oz) desiccated coconut
½ teaspoon baking powder
2 eggs, beaten
25 g (1 oz) glacé cherries, chopped
50 g (2 oz) chopped mixed candied peel
1 tablespoon cornflour
3 tablespoons lemon curd

Preparation time: 20 minutes
Cooking time: 2 hours

This pudding is so called because of the 'gold nuggets' hidden in the centre! If you don't want to freeze the pineapple juice from the can use a small bottle of juice to make the sauce.

1. Drain the pineapple, reserving the juice. Cut two rings into wedges, and chop the rest finely.
2. Put the chopped pineapple into a bowl and add the margarine, sugar, flour, coconut, baking powder, eggs, cherries and peel. Stir together until well mixed to a soft consistency. If too stiff add a little milk.
3. Spoon a little more than half the mixture into a well-buttered 900 ml (1½ pint) pudding basin. Make a hollow in the centre and fill with the pineapple wedges. Cover with the rest of the mixture, spreading it evenly.
To Freeze: Cover with buttered greaseproof paper and foil and seal well over the edge of the basin. Freeze. Freeze the pineapple juice separately.
To Serve: Allow the pudding and juice to thaw in the refrigerator for 6 hours. Place the pudding basin in a saucepan of boiling water and steam for 2 hours. Make the pineapple juice up to 300 ml (½ pint) with water. Blend with the cornflour and cook over a gentle heat, stirring, until thickened. Stir in the lemon curd. Serve this sauce hot with the pudding.

RHUBARB GINGER EVE

350 g (12 oz) rhubarb
50 g (2 oz) soft brown sugar
Sponge:
50 g (2 oz) soft margarine
25 g (1 oz) soft brown sugar
1 tablespoon black treacle
100 g (4 oz) self-raising flour, sifted
1½ teaspoons ground ginger
¼ teaspoon baking powder
1 egg, beaten
4 tablespoons milk

Preparation time: 15 minutes
Cooking time: 50-60 minutes
Oven: 180°C, 350°F, Gas Mark 4

This recipe is a variation of the well loved Eve's Pudding, which combines apples with a sponge topping. The sponge bakes to a light texture with a crunchy surface that contrasts so well with the soft fruit filling. It is a very simple dessert to make, the sponge ingredients are beaten together in a matter of minutes.

1. Remove the leaves, if any, from the rhubarb and trim the stems. Cut into 2.5 cm (1 inch) pieces.
2. Put the rhubarb into a 900 ml (1½ pint) freezerproof pie dish with the brown sugar.
3. Put all the sponge ingredients into a bowl and beat together until smooth. Spread over the rhubarb to cover it evenly.
To Freeze: Cover and freeze.
To Serve: Allow to thaw for 3 hours. Uncover and put into a preheated oven. Cook for 50-60 minutes or until the sponge is risen and firm to the touch. Serve hot with cream or custard.

Variation:
Omit the treacle and ginger from the sponge and add the grated rind of a large orange. Using a small sharp knife, remove the bitter white pith, chop the flesh and mix with the rhubarb. Prepare and cook the pudding in the same way.

CLOCKWISE FROM THE FRONT: Rhubarb ginger eve; Homely bread pudding; Treasure island pudding

HONEY APPLE STRUDEL

Makes 16 slices
1 egg
150 ml (¼ pint) water
300 g (11 oz) plain flour, sifted
Filling:
1 kg (2 lb) cooking apples, peeled, cored and finely chopped
40 g (1½ oz) crushed wheat flakes
4 tablespoons clear honey
½ teaspoon ground cinnamon
50 g (2 oz) walnuts, chopped
100 g (4 oz) butter, melted
sifted icing sugar, to serve

Preparation time: 30 minutes
Cooking time: 30 minutes, plus reheating
Oven: 190°C, 375°F, Gas Mark 5

1. Beat together the egg and water. Add the flour and mix to make a slightly sticky dough.
2. Turn the dough on to a lightly floured board. Throw the dough on to the board repeatedly with flicking wrist movements for about 5 minutes. This will make it smooth and elastic. Then knead lightly for a further 3 minutes.
3. Put the dough in a lightly floured bowl, cover with cling film and leave to rest for 10 minutes.
4. Meanwhile, mix together the apples, cereal, honey, cinnamon and nuts with 1 tablespoon of the butter.
5. Divide the dough in half (wrap the part not being used in cling film to prevent it drying). Roll out the dough on a lightly floured surface to a rectangle about 50 x 30 cm (20 x 12 inches). To stretch the dough to this size rectangle you may find it easier to pull it gently with floured hands, using stroking movements, instead of using a rolling pin.
6. Cut the rectangle in half lengthways. Brush each strip with melted butter and spread evenly with half the filling. Fold in a 1 cm (½ inch) margin down each long side, then roll up from a long edge. Repeat with the rest of the dough.
7. Put on a lightly greased baking sheet, brush with melted butter and put into a preheated oven. Bake for 25-30 minutes or until lightly coloured. Cool.
To Freeze: Open freeze, then wrap in foil.
To Serve: Allow to thaw at room temperature for 2 hours. To serve hot, unwrap, place on a baking sheet and reheat in a preheated oven (190°C, 375°F, Gas Mark 5) for 20 minutes. Slice, dredge with icing sugar and serve with whipped cream.

BANANA PUFFS WITH APRICOT PURÉE

1 x 215 g (7½ oz) packet frozen puff pastry, thawed
2 large bananas
oil for deep frying
100 g (4 oz) caster sugar
1 x 225 g (8 oz) can apricots, drained

Preparation time: 25 minutes
Cooking time: 10 minutes

Deep-fried puff pastry is delicious and different. Make sure the oil is hot enough – it is best to check this with a sugar thermometer – so that the puffs cook quickly. They may spit a little if the pastry opens slightly during the frying so, for safety, keep young children well away.

1. Roll out the pastry dough to a rectangle 41 x 31 cm (16½ x 12½ inches) and trim the edge. Cut into 16 strips each 30 x 2.5 cm (12 x 1 inch).
2. Peel the bananas and cut each in half lengthways, then crossways into quarters, making 16 pieces.
3. Brush one strip of pastry with water. Place a piece of banana on top and wind the strip around it to enclose it completely, sealing the ends well. Repeat with the rest of the pastry strips and bananas.
To Freeze: Lay the pieces on a baking sheet and open freeze until firm, then pack in a rigid freezer container.
To Serve: Allow the banana puffs to thaw at room temperature for 30 minutes. Fry in four batches, of four puffs each, in hot oil (190°C, 375°F or when a cube of bread rises instantly to the surface) for 1-2 minutes or until lightly golden. Drain on paper towels, sprinkle with the caster sugar and keep hot. Purée the apricots in an electric blender and serve as a sauce with the hot banana puffs. Dilute the purée with a little juice from the apricot can if necessary.

Variation:
Use fresh pineapple instead of bananas. Cut the pineapple into slices, trim off the outer skin and cut out the central core. Cut each ring into 4 pieces. Wrap in the pastry as above. Sprinkle the pineapple puffs with the caster sugar mixed with 1 teaspoon powdered ginger and serve with a Caramel Sauce (page 70).

Honey apple strudel; Shoo-fly pie; Banana puffs with apricot purée

SHOO-FLY PIE

Serves 6
175 g (6 oz) shortcrust pastry
Filling:
100 g (4 oz) molasses
50 g (2 oz) dark soft brown sugar
1 egg, beaten
3 tablespoons boiling water
Crumb topping:
150 g (5 oz) flour
pinch of salt
¼ teaspoon baking powder
¼ teaspoon cream of tartar
50 g (2 oz) margarine
25 g (1 oz) caster sugar

Preparation time: 25 minutes
Cooking time: 40-45 minutes
Oven: 230°C, 450°F, Gas Mark 8;
180°C, 350°F, Gas Mark 4

The name for this Pennsylvanian speciality is derived from the fact that cooks had to shoo away the flies that would buzz around the molasses while the pies were being prepared.

1. Roll out the pastry dough and use to line a 20 cm (8 inch) flan tin. Chill while preparing the filling.
2. To make the filling, stir together all the ingredients until smoothly blended.
3. Sift the flour, salt, baking powder and cream of tartar into a bowl. Rub in the margarine until the mixture resembles fine crumbs. Stir in the sugar.
4. Pour the filling into the prepared pastry case and sprinkle over the crumb topping evenly.
To Freeze: Open freeze. When solid, wrap in foil and store.
To Serve: Allow to thaw for 2 hours. Unwrap and place on a baking sheet in a preheated oven. Bake for 15 minutes. Reduce the heat and bake for a further 25 minutes or until lightly browned. Serve warm with whipped cream.

INDEX

PDO 83-204